English National Opera Guide

The Magic Flute

Mozart

English National Opera
receives financial
assistance from the Arts
Council of Great Britain
and the Greater London
Council.

Backstage at Weimar during one of the twenty performances of the opera under Goethe's management (1794). (Photo: Int. Stiftung Mozarteum, Salzburg).

Preface

English National Opera Guides are intended to be companions to opera in performance. They contain articles and illustrations relevant to any production and not only those mounted by English National Opera. Of general interest, also, is the inclusion of the complete original libretto of the opera, side by side with an English translation. There are many reasons why sung words may not be clearly distinguishable, whatever the language and however excellent the performance. The composer may have set several lines of text together, for instance, or he may have demanded an orchestral sound through which no voice can clearly articulate. ENO Guides supply English readers with an opportunity to know a libretto in advance and so greatly increase their understanding and enjoyment of performances whether live, broadcast or recorded.

ENO is very grateful to The Stock Exchange for sponsoring this Guide to *The Magic Flute*. Such sponsorship is an indication of a steadily growing public interest in opera, and we hope the Guides will prove useful to new and experienced opera-lovers alike. An audience which knows what to look and listen for — one that demands a high standard of performance and recognises it when it is achieved — is our best support and, of course, an assurance for the future of opera in the English-speaking world.

Nicholas John
Editor

3

The Magic Flute

Wolfgang Amadeus Mozart

English National Opera Guides Series Editor:
Nicholas John

This Guide is sponsored by The Stock Exchange

John Calder ● London
Riverrun Press ● New York

First published in Great Britain, 1980, by
John Calder (Publishers) Ltd.,
18 Brewer Street,
London W1R 4AS
and
in the U.S.A., 1980, by
Riverrun Press Inc.,
175 Fifth Avenue,
New York, NY 10010

ISBN 0 7145 3768 3 Paperback edition

BRITISH LIBRARY CATALOGUING DATA

Schikaneder, Emanuel
   The magic flute. — (English National Opera
   guides; 3).
   1. Operas — To 1800 — Librettos
   I. Title   II. Giesecke, Karl Ludwig
   III. John, Nicholas   IV. Geliot, Michael
   V. Besch, Anthony   VI. Mozart, Wolfgang Amadeus
   VII. Series
   782.1'2   ML50.M939

Typeset in Plantin by Alan Sutton Publishing Limited, Gloucester
Printed by Whitstable Litho Ltd in Great Britain.

Contents

List of Illustrations

Introduction

In 1791, Mozart, at the age of 35, found himself with little work, out of favour at the court of the new Emperor, Leopold II, and bound to support a growing family and a pregnant young wife. (Nor was his own health strong, since he suffered, putting a brave face on the matter, from a serious liver complaint.) In the spring, he wrote several curiosities: a piece for a mechanical clock and a Rondo to display the virtuoso talents of a blind girl who played the glass harmonica. Yet, no doubt feeling time hang heavily (for him) on his hands, he also agreed to collaborate on an opera with an old friend, a very experienced man of the theatre, called Emmanuel Schikaneder. Schikaneder had first won a reputation touring the Empire with a troupe who performed low comedy and Shakespeare on alternate nights — he had himself been a celebrated Hamlet.

The subject of the collaboration was to include parts for Schikaneder (Papageno) and his company which included Mozart's friend, Benedict Schack (Tamino), and Josefa Hofer his sister-in-law (The Queen of the Night). It was to please the public with a story using the fashionable theme of magic as a pretext for spectacular stage effects in Schikaneder's little wooden theatre on the outskirts of Vienna. And it was to be cast in the popular form of Viennese entertainment known as *Singspiel,* in which the music was interspersed with dialogue in German.

In July, while composing *The Magic Flute,* Mozart received an anonymous commission for a Requiem. He continued to work on both scores together until August when he had to stop entirely to meet an important and very urgent request. This was for an opera to celebrate the coronation of Leopold as King of Bohemia in early September. The form of opera approved by the court for such an occasion was the *opera seria* and Mozart chose an old libretto by Metastasio, the greatest master of libretti for that genre. He and his wife Constanze had to travel to Prague, where in three weeks he completed, rehearsed and conducted the first performance of *La Clemenza di Tito.* The opera pleased the press, which noted the circumstances of the composition and Mozart's ill health, but was received by the new Empress with the comment *'una porcheria tedesca'* — German boorishness. With the fee of 200 gulden in his pocket, Mozart immediately returned to Vienna to complete his score for Schikaneder. The major part of the work must have been ready by then but the overture and March of the Priests were finished only days before the First Night (September 30). Mozart always composed his overtures last and the March may well have been added to assist the staging.

The First Night audience responded with increasing enthusiasm, and particularly liked the scenic effects. Schikaneder repeated it,

Mozart by Doris Stock

although Mozart only conducted one other performance, and during October and November it became a resounding success.

Mozart was by this time hurrying to complete the Requiem, which he had superstitiously come to believe was due for his own funeral. He also completed an aria, a concert piece for basset horn, a clarinet concerto and a Masonic march for the opening of a new lodge. So, at the same time as he was composing a *Singspiel*, he was also working on an opera in the most conventional and elitist form of the period and, while conceiving scores for several Masonic subjects, he was preparing a Catholic Mass. By the end of November, however, ill health forced him to retire to his bed, from where he desperately followed the continuing success of *The Magic Flute*. Constanze, who had been in Baden taking the waters for her health, rejoined him. On December 4, family and friends rehearsed part of the as yet unfinished Requiem at his bedside. Early the next morning, he died, to be buried in a pauper's grave.

Synopsis

This summary of the plot of *The Magic Flute* may be of help in discussing the opera, and recalling the sequence of scenes.

Act One

Tamino, a prince, is saved from a serpent by Three Ladies, attendant on the Queen of the Night. She promises her daughter,

Schikaneder's production Act One, scene one in a coloured engraving by Josef and Peter Schaffer, 1795. (Historisches Museum der Stadt Wien)

Pamina, to him if he will rescue her from Sarastro, whom she calls a wicked demon. Tamino agrees and sets off in the company of the Queen's birdcatcher, a child of nature called Papageno. They each take a magic present (Tamino has a flute, his companion some bells) and they are to be guided by Three Boys in a flying machine.

Pamina is recaptured by Sarastro's Moorish servant, Monostatos, after she has unsuccessfully tried to escape. Papageno, separated on the journey from Tamino, frightens Monostatos so much that he is able to help Pamina escape successfully.

Tamino is convinced by one of Sarastro's followers that Sarastro's principles are virtuous and wise. Pamina and Papageno are discovered by Sarastro as they flee. Tamino and Papageno are invited to undertake the initiation trials of Sarastro's circle.

Act Two

Sarastro thanks his priests for agreeing to allow the two strangers to undertake the trials.

(*First Trial*) Tamino and Papageno are sworn to silence in a darkened room. They resist the temptation to talk to the Three Ladies. Monostatos, about to embrace Pamina, overhears the Queen of the Night swear vengeance on Sarastro, telling Pamina to kill him and bring back to her the Circle of the Sun, which he was given by Pamina's father. Monostatos threatens Pamina when the Queen has vanished but Sarastro intervenes and dismisses him forever from his service.

(*Second Trial*) Tamino and Papageno are still sworn to silence. An old crone easily attracts Papageno's attention but Tamino refuses to greet Pamina, to her infinite sadness. Sarastro then announces that the Second Trial is overcome and that Tamino must now bid Pamina farewell. Papageno tells the old woman that he loves her truly and she is transformed into his perfect female counterpart, Papagena, before they too are forced to part.

Pamina's grief drives her to contemplate suicide which the Three Boys prevent by telling her that Tamino still loves her. She joins Tamino, and together they pass through the (*Third and Fourth*) *Trials of Fire and Water*, as he plays the flute. They enter Sarastro's temple.

The Three Boys then advise Papageno not to hang himself but to use his bells to recover Papagena. The couple are joyfully reunited.

The Queen, her Ladies and Monostatos plot to infiltrate Sarastro's temple. They vanish before the sunlight of wisdom and truth which shines around Sarastro, the Three Boys, the lovers and the priests.

Note

The numbers which appear in square brackets throughout the text refer to the numbered Thematic Guide on pages 51-58.

'Singspiel' and Symbolism

Rodney Milnes

When first performed in 1791, *The Magic Flute* was described in three different ways. The playbill announced *Eine grosse Oper* — 'a grand opera'; the published libretto referred to it as a *Singspiel*; and in his personal catalogue Mozart entered it as a 'German opera'. It is, of course, all three and more. As the playbill promised, it is grander than the term *Singspiel* would have suggested to prospective audiences, and although the adjective 'German' had special significance for Mozart, who for most of his working life sought to re-create a national school of opera — and here succeeded — the score nevertheless contains elements of Italian operatic form, significantly those associated with the Queen of the Night, a character symbolising reaction. And its universality wholly transcends any nationalist designation.

It is impossible to separate *Singspiel* — literally 'song-play' — from other vernacular nationalist operatic schools in conflict with and reaction to the almost complete dominance of Italian opera in Europe that lasted from the end of the seventeenth century for almost a hundred years. One common feature was, of course, spoken dialogue in place of sung recitative. English ballad operas following in the wake of *The Beggar's Opera* (1728), itself a direct counterblast to Handelian *opera seria*, were translated into German and proved immensely popular. *Opéra-comique* survived the Italianization of French opera by Lully and his successors and became the dominant school following the decline of Rameau. Composers of *Singspiel* studied with profit the techniques of French popular opera rather than those of Italian *opera buffa* (three characteristics, strophic song in place of *da-capo* forms, the rondeau, and the vaudeville finale, found their way into both Mozart's German and Italian operas). The common feature of all three is that they represented popular lyric entertainment as opposed to official, court-based Italian opera.

The ancestors of popular opera are many: fairground entertainments and mystery plays; cantatas in costume (a form that flourished in Leipzig where, confusingly, they were sometimes designated *dramma per musica*); school operas and before them liturgical drama, stretching far back into the middle ages and the Byzantine era; perhaps the English 'Jigg', a sung and danced postlude to, or interlude during, a serious play — for example, the finale to the rustics' 'Pyramus and Thisbe' in *A Midsummer Night's Dream* — at first improvised, later written down; this *commedia dell'arte*-type affair relates backwards to the classical Greek satyr play and forwards to the Italian *intermezzo*, direct ancestor of *opera buffa*.

11

The term *Singspiel* seems first to have been used in 1698 to describe the performance in German of a French opera by the Italian Lully given in Stuttgart, in which recitative was replaced by dialogue. In Hamburg, serious operas were given with dialogue, sometimes with the arias in Italian as a sop to establishment taste, until 1739; the free Hanseatic city was the last bastion of repertory vernacular opera. From then on Italian *opera seria* won the day and popular musical entertainment took to the road. Schikaneder's was just one of many touring companies giving both drama and *Singspiel*. Although *Singspiel* was never exclusively comic — Goethe wrote many librettos, and in the 1770s we find 'serious', even 'tragic' *Singspiele* announced — it was by and large a light-hearted affair.

In Vienna, capital of the Empire and of *opera seria*, it was very light-hearted indeed. Subjects were exotic; while *opera seria* and Gluckian reform opera went to the classical world for their subject matter, *Singspiele* (not to mention *opéra-comique*) went one further, to the East; against the interest in classicism born in the seventeenth century was set the first translation of the *1,001 Nights* in the early 1700s. Indeed, Viennese popular theatre in the 1780s must have looked a little like a London season in which pantomimes lasted the year round, an indigestible diet of *Aladdins* and *Ali Babas*. Joseph II's attempt to found a National, or German, Opera in 1778 failed, though its repertory did include Mozart's *Die Entführung aus dem Serail*, in which a *Singspiel* text was allied to music that aimed rather higher, perhaps justifying the Emperor's famous criticism of 'too many notes, my dear Mozart'. Mozart's involvement with *Singspiel*, or near-*Singspiel*, also produced *Der Schauspieldirektor* (more a play with music), *Thämos, König von Ägypten* (definitely a play with music), and the unfinished *Zaide*, in which he used *mélodrame*, or dialogue spoken over music, a technique exploited by the *Singspiel* composer Benda, much admired by Mozart, later used by Weber (*Der Freischütz*), Beethoven (*Fidelio* and *Egmont*), Schubert (*Zauberharfe*), and thereafter seldom until Strauss (*Die Frau ohne Schatten*) and Britten (*Gloriana*); it was, however, the mainstay of popular nineteenth-century theatre in England and the golden age of Hollywood.

Although the roots of *The Magic Flute* are in *Singspiel*, the score transcended the form. Admired by and influential upon great German opera composers who followed, it spawned such works as *Fidelio* and *Freischütz*, technically speaking 'serious' *Singspiele*, before *Singspiel* reverted to comic subjects and changed its name to *Spieloper*. French *opéra-comique*, the other pollinator of that glorious hybrid *Fidelio*, continued to use dialogue (except that successful examples, like *Faust*, were promptly turned into 'respectable' *grand opéra*) until *Carmen* went as far as the form could go. Opera with dialogue is scarcely written any more, much to opera's loss. Dialogue does save *so* much time.

When *The Magic Flute* was first performed at the Theater auf der Wieden, a temporary wooden theatre in the suburbs of Vienna with a capacity of 1,000, audiences may have been expecting another pantomime-like *Singspiel*, a fairy story with many magic effects, which at one level is what they got. The piece was an instant success, as was Mozart's previous German opera, *Die Entführung*, and as were his Italian comedies when performed anywhere other than Vienna. But there was more to the *Flute* than fairy tale, and Mozart himself became impatient at one performance when a boorish Bavarian visitor laughed in the wrong places and plainly did not understand what was going on. Mozart called him a Papageno. The fact that there obviously was something more to the work has given rise over the years to innumerable theories as to exactly what that something was. In 1866 Moritz Zille told the world that Tamino represented the Emperor Joseph II, Pamina the Austrian people, the Queen the reactionary Empress Maria Theresa, Monostatos the Jesuits, etc. etc.. While it may have been obvious from the beginning that much of the ritual in the second act was that of Freemasonry — obvious, certainly, to Masons — it was only at the beginning of this century that it came to be discussed openly, when it gave rise to the famous theory of the (non-existant) change of plot. To examine this we must return to the sources.

The first, though marginal, source was *Lulu, oder die Zauberflöte*, a story by A.J. Liebeskind, one of a collection of pseudo-oriental fairy tales edited by C.M. Wieland and published in 1786 under the title of *Dschinnistan*. This book was raided for countless *Singspiele* both at Schikaneder's theatre (among them Wranitzky's *Oberon*, 1789) and at his rival Marinelli's Kärntnertortheater. While the *Flute* was being written, Marinelli staged *Kaspar the Bassoon-player, or the Magic Zither*, with music by Wenzel Müller and also loosely based on *Lulu*. It is said that fearful of accusations of plagiarism, Mozart and Schikaneder suddenly changed their *Lulu* plot half way through the first act. Plagiarism hardly entered into it: it was rife in the Viennese theatre of the day, and it would make as much sense to say that a Palladium *Aladdin* plagiarised one at the Players Theatre. Commentators may have felt the need to propose the change-of-plot theory because in the story the good fairy Perifeme gives Prince Lulu (thank heavens the name was changed) a magic flute, amongst other things, to rescue her daughter Sidi from the evil magician Dilsengbuin, which he eventually does. In the opera, theorists maintain, the Queen starts as a good character and Sarastro as a bad one, then suddenly the positions are reversed. Is this really tenable if you listen carefully to the Queen's music? It is as unwise to believe everything people say in the theatre as it is in real life, especially if in the middle of a *Singspiel* they suddenly loose off into a torrent of *opera seria* coloratura. In any event, Mozart saw *Kaspar* and dismissed it as worthless.

13

There is another far more significant source of the *Flute*: the Abbé Terrasson's *Sethos*, published in 1731 as a historic treatise on the mysteries of Isis and Osiris and accepted as such until well into the nineteenth century, but in fact a clever forgery and no more than a novel. Sethos was supposedly an Egyptian Prince, and the Queen in *Flute* has the characteristics of his mother-in-law Daluca rather than of Liebeskind's Perifeme. Also from *Sethos* come the text recited by the Armed Men, the Three Ladies, the serpent, the trials of fire and water, and the ritual of the second act. *Sethos* had already been mined for material for *Thämos*, for *Der Stein der Weisen* (libretto by Schikaneder, music by Benedict Schack, later the first Tamino), and for pieces at Marinelli's theatre. The Three Boys, incidentally, come from another story in *Dschinnistan*, and Papageno, designed primarily as a star role for Schikaneder, is a mixture of Kasperle, a Viennese Mr Punch crossed with Merry Andrew, and the *commedia dell'arte* characters popular at the Kärntnertortheater.

So there is no single source for the *Flute* libretto, and there was probably more than one librettist, although as claimants only emerged after the deaths of Mozart and Schikaneder it is impossible to know the truth of this (I am inclined to disbelieve Giesecke's opportunist claim to authorship made in a Viennese restaurant in 1818). But the main source was *Sethos*, a Masonic text, and the rituals were those of Freemasonry, which gave rise to the second change-of-plot theory. This is based on the official suppression of the sect in Vienna after the death of Joseph II, himself a member, and proposes that half way through composition Mozart and Schikaneder, also both Masons, abandoned the fairy tale and turned the *Flute* into, if not propaganda, then at least a morale-booster for their beleaguered brothers. The turning point is supposed to come with Tamino's encounter with the Speaker, and thence the reversal of the Queen's and Sarastro's roles. This theory seems most unlikely on countless grounds: would Mozart, after all that he had achieved, bother to write a simple fairy-tale, even for ready money? Had there not been enough, if not orthodox Masonic, then at least esoteric entertainments, some written by Mozart himself, for them to count as a sub-genre of *Singspiel*? Is the association of night with good and day with evil likely in eighteenth century terms? The idea crumbles once the Masonic symbolism of the libretto is fully explained.

This has at least been done by Jacques Chailley in his exhaustively researched and presumably massively indiscreet *The Magic Flute, Masonic Opera*. Among his many revelations, and they are no less than that, is the existence of controversy in eighteenth-century Masonic circles over whether or not women should be admitted as full members. There were Lodges of Adoption for women, and female initiates took the name of the Order of Mopsos. Among the items in their ritual were a serpent, veils, and a golden padlock. The libretto is thus bristling with Masonic symbols long before the appearance of the Speaker, and the plot is nothing so simple as a matter of 'good' Masons being threatened by a 'bad' Maria Theresa, or whoever. They are all in the same game, and there is no reason why a 'bad' Queen should not be handing out 'good' symbols like a flute and a chime of bells.

The conflict in the *Flute* between the Queen and Sarastro for control of the Circle of the Sun symbolises the conflict in Masonic lore between the dualism proposed by inscriptions on the twin pillars of Hiram's Temple of Solomon, which list various opposing forces: Masculine/Feminine, Sun/Moon, Day/Night, Fire/Water, Gold/Silver etc. etc.. Note here that the Three Boys carry silver (lunar) palms (solar) at their first entry, suggesting that they are above and beyond the dualism, and thus perfect beings. The Queen seeks to perpetuate the conflict by seizing the Circle of the Sun worn by her late husband, Sarastro's predecessor, and institute her own reign. Sarastro's aim is to resolve the conflict by creating in Tamino and Pamina 'the new pair' he sings of in 'Oh, Isis and Osiris'* (Aria with Chorus No. 10). The synthesis of all the warring elements will herald a new, golden age of peace and wisdom. He does not have the unconditional support of his priests, who voice many of the anti-feminist sentiments that must have been expressed in eighteenth-century Masonic circles. Whether or not Sarastro's plan is orthodox Masonry a non-Mason cannot tell (and it is one of the few beans that Professor Chailley does not spill), but in creating Pamina, a woman who joins Tamino for his most dangerous trials, who 'is not afraid of night or death, is worthy and will be accepted', and who sings 'Wherever you go I will be at your side, I myself will lead you as love leads me', Mozart was definitely on the side of the non-Masonic angels, as he was in *'Bei Männern'*, Duet No. 7 [14], with its promise that 'man and woman, woman and man' (the reversal surely not just in the interests of rhyme) 'together attain divinity'. (Schikaneder, incidentally, was a lapsed Mason. An eighteenth-century constitution excluded 'slaves, women, and immoral men' in that order. Schikaneder fell into the last category.)

Professor Chailley's book is extremely complicated, and like all decipherers he sometimes overstates his case, but he does show that far from being just a pantomine or, in E.J. Dent's magnificently orotund phrase, 'one of the most absurd specimens of that form of literature in which absurdity is regarded as a matter of course', the *Flute* libretto is a tightly organised text, its symbolism logically worked out. He explains the various trials, the 'initial swoon' that Pamina and Tamino both undergo and that Papageno parodies, and such details as why the flute and bells are taken away at the beginning of the second act. It is, for example, perfectly logical that two

* Sarastro's reference is arguably to Tamino and Papageno, not Pamina, since they are the two profane ones to be initiated at that stage — Editor.

15

of the characters, Papageno and Monostatos, start out on the wrong sides and move across during the action. Papageno works in the woman's world, but joins Tamino and the priests — note how often his priest-mentor says 'be a *man*'. Monostatos logically joins the forces of darkness. His blackness, incidentally, is not necessarily of skin. He represents the black-magician Siosiri, the Judas-figure of Masonic lore who assassinated the architect Hiram and is descended from the raven that brought bad news back to the ark; Monostatos refers to Pamina as his 'dove', the bird that brought the good news — again, no coincidence.

Although there is a certain satisfaction in seeing everything in the *Flute* slot neatly into place, full understanding of the relevant ritual is certainly not essential to the appreciation of what remains a Masonic opera. It describes a journey from darkness to light, and celebrates the possibility of progress. 'Soon superstition will vanish and wisdom triumph; come, Peace, and fill the hearts of men, so that earth will become a paradise and mortal men as the gods themselves', sing the Boys with touching optimism at the start of the finale. That in a nutshell is what the *Flute* is about. After nearly two hundred years humanity seems no nearer that goal.

Tamino attracts wild beasts with his flute-playing in Schikaneder's 1795 production. (*Historisches Museum der Stadt Wien*)

A Vision of Reconciliation
David Cairns

For an opera that the general public took to its heart from the beginning and that great poets from Goethe to Auden have revered, *The Magic Flute* has had a strangely grudging press; critics have often been reluctant to take its message seriously. Even now we may sometimes hear it described as sublime music unhappily married to a foolish and vulgar plot, whose text is mere hot air when it isn't juvenile. The sophisticated may even complain, privately, that the music itself with all its beauties is lacking in the rich ironies and ambiguities of *Don Giovanni* and *Così fan tutte*. According to these critics, the work marks a reversion by Mozart to a more primitive genre of opera, in which the composer is no longer in undisputed control of the dramatic machinery, and the musical numbers regularly give way to the spoken word; a genre, too, in which the complex, living individuals of the great Italian comedies are replaced by the two-dimensional stereotypes of contemporary Viennese pantomime. In this view *The Magic Flute* is great in spite of the libretto and solely because of the music; but not even Mozart's genius can turn it into a serious and coherent work of art.

Thus the very simplicity of the work becomes a barrier to an understanding of it. Our way of looking at Mozart is still tinged, unconsciously, with the nineteenth-century view of him as a purely instinctive genius and child of nature who was not really aware of what he did. As a result we fail to realise the extent to which Mozart was consciously in charge, shaping his material to clearly formulated ends. It is always a mistake to make a lot of the formal sources of his mature compositions. He takes his models from what he finds around him, the conventional art of the day, but uses them to create something personal to himself, unique, and coherent. Nowhere more so than in *The Magic Flute*. The more we study it the more unmistakably it is seen to embody a consistent plan.

The simplicity of the music is indeed remarkable: simplicity of form, style, material. It is Mozart's most transparent operatic score, melodically the most direct, harmonically the most pure and unadorned (its chromatic inflexions being always contained within a clear diatonic framework), in texture the most luminous. Yet it is a positive simplicity, subtle and purposeful, seemingly uncomplicated in its effect, profoundly artful in the means used to achieve it — the musician's super-sensitive response to the drama, which at every turn is articulated by the musical form and expression. To consider only the orchestration: we think of it as plainer than that of Mozart's other operas; yet hardly two out of the forty-odd separate or linked movements that make up the work are scored for the same forces. This is something only slightly connected with the presence of unusual instruments: trombones, basset-horns and glockenspiel (the latter two appearing in only a handful of numbers). The conventional instruments of the operatic orchestra are handled with a marvellous diversity to reflect each shift of mood or feeling or atmosphere.

Mozart's consummate dramatic sense is seen above all in the profound unity-in-diversity of the work's musical style, reflecting that of the action and symbolised by the magic flute itself, the instrument created by Osiris from a shepherd's multiple pipes — the many resolved into the one. There is a single 'Magic Flute style', a synthesis, like the drama itself, of widely differing elements: Viennese vernacular song, Italian bravura aria and buffo ensemble, chorale, fugue, ritual chorus, extended accompanied recitative; learned and popular, sacred and profane, spirit and earth. It is the musical analogue of the drama's high theme of reconciliation.

The theme of *The Magic Flute*: there can no longer be any doubt as to its seriousness, and its deliberate and systematic Masonic connotations and Mozart's central involvement in the plan. *The Magic Flute* is a conscious document of **Freemasonry,** an affirmation of faith in its mysteries and its beliefs. But **Freemasonry** is a language for encoding philosophical ideas and spiritual aspirations that are common to many religions; its forms may be esoteric, their content is open to all and concerns mankind. We do not have to be able to read all the signs in order to receive the message of the work. Its essential meaning is immediately clear (though we may never exhaust its meaningfulness). Mozart does not disdain to use the vulgar medium of popular comedy for his parable of the purification of the human soul. Like Shakespeare, like the men who devised the old miracle plays, he sees no incongruity — rather, a fitness. 'Except ye become as little children . . .'

Overture.

The Overture is in E flat (a key whose three flats gave it special significance for Masons). It prepares us for what is to come, with its solemn, momentous introduction (*Adagio*) [1a] leading through tension and uncertainty — throbbing syncopations, harmonic darkenings — to the jubilant polyphony of the *Allegro* [2]. Half way through, the *Allegro* is interrupted by the three-fold wind chord [1b], which in Act Two will summon the postulants at various stages of the initiation. Its effect, in the Overture, is to check the *Allegro*'s confident energy. The strings discuss it in an anxious *sotto voce*, and the music moves through a dark series of minor keys before — the clarinets leading — the orchestra sees its way ahead once more and, instrument by instrument, rushes with joyful eagerness back to E flat major.

From the outset the glow of trombones colours the orchestral sound. Predominantly ecclesiastical instruments in Mozart's time, here they play not just in a scene or two, for special effect (as they do in *Idomeneo* and *Don Giovanni*), but in fully a quarter of the work — one sign among many that this is not a conventional *Singspiel* but a sacred comedy. If (as Jacques Chailley claims) the note-pattern of the opening bars of the Overture — three resounding chords plus the upbeat to the second and the third chord — is meant to be heard as a group of five, that is only appropriate. Five represents Woman in Masonic number-symbolism (five-note figures are prominent in the work in scenes that take place in or under the influence of the feminine domain); and the regeneration of Woman — who in Freemasonry embodies the emotional, instinctive, unreasoning, 'inferior' half of the human psyche — is central to the work. Her progress, in the person of Pamina, becomes the focal point; in the end it is Pamina who, by her fully awakened love, will lead Tamino on the final stage of their journey. This was a bold step by Mozart and Schikaneder. Women were not admitted by orthodox Masonry to full enlightenment, and it must have caused rumblings among the brotherhood. Indeed there is a suggestion in Act Two scene 21 that the priests are taken aback by the novelty of Sarastro's grand design.

Act One

No. 1 Introduction: TAMINO, THREE LADIES.

A rocky, mountainous terrain, with woods and a temple. Tamino, a prince from foreign lands, is being pursued by a huge serpent. He cannot defend himself: he has a bow but no arrows. In forty graphic bars the music depicts his breathless flight and the heaving coils of the approaching snake: a tense, rushing C minor, with strong contrasts of dynamics, stabbing offbeat accents, and lurid chords on woodwind and horns [3]. As the serpent reaches him, Tamino falls to the ground in a faint; but at the same moment three women, servants of the Queen of the Night, wearing black veils and armed with silver spears, come out of the temple and kill the monster. The music swerves, via A flat major, into E flat as they congratulate themselves on their noble deed. Mock heroic fanfares and violin semiquavers parading up and down the scale betray the Ladies' self-importance, but the key of E flat is significant. Tamino's loss of consciousness is to be the start of a new existence for him. It will be paralleled a few scenes later when Pamina, too, faints after an attack by animal nature. For each of them this symbolic death is the precondition of rebirth into the life of the spirit; though neither of them realises it, it is the beginning of a pilgrimage that will lead them, after many trials, to each other's arms and to the threshold of the golden age.

For the present, Tamino is very much in the land of unenlightenment, the domain of ignorance and unregenerate Woman.

The Three Ladies are frivolous, vain, sensual, and of strictly limited understanding; their musical characterisation is quite explicit. They are smitten with the beauty of Tamino, and each longs to be left alone with him and tries desperately to make the other two go away [4], until they realise that they are all three thinking the same thing, whereupon they become almost hysterical with jealousy and frustration. In the end they bid the still unconscious youth a tender farewell [5] and go back into the temple to tell the Queen about him. The music of this whole Trio is at once irresistibly comic and exquisitely beautiful in a luminous, airy way that we will recognise as characteristic of *The Magic Flute*.

Tamino comes to himself to find the serpent dead at his feet. While he is staring at it in amazement he hears pan-pipes from nearby [6]; and a moment later a strange figure, a man, yet covered in feathers like a bird and carrying on his back a cage full of birds, comes into the clearing.

No. 2 Aria PAPAGENO.

Papageno's first aria, [7] in a bright G major, with flowing semiquavers alternating with hopping, birdlike rhythms and intervals, has the folksong-like freshness and open-hearted good humour which will typify his music throughout the opera. The third verse was apparently an afterthought — a wise one (quite apart from the Masonic associations of the magic number three!):

An early design for Papageno
(Bibliothèque Nationale,
Music Department, Paris)

the tune is too good to be heard only twice, and the third verse clinches the effect of the first two. Papageno, ever keen to talk about himself, tells us how he lures birds with his pipes and catches them in traps. If only he had a girl-trap, he would catch girls and the one he liked best would be his wife.

The ensuing conversation between Tamino and Pagageno is long and written in traditional 'low' pantomime style. It is drastically shortened in many productions, but it serves several purposes: to impart a good deal of necessary information, to characterise the relationship — a variant of the archetypal master-and-servant — which will link the two men until their parallel but separate destinies diverge in the final scenes of the opera, and to establish the identity of the bird-catcher as uncorrupted Natural Man. Papageno works for the Queen of the Night, receiving food and drink in return for the birds he brings her. In the uncut version of the dialogue he does not actually claim that he slew the serpent, so much as fall in readily with Tamino's assumption that he did. Immediately the Three Ladies return: 'Papageno, no wine for you today, only water, no sugarbread but a stone!' And instead of sweet figs they laughingly present him with a padlock, and lock his mouth as a punishment for lying. Papageno is reduced to doleful dumbshow. Before they go the Ladies give the Prince a present from the Queen — a portrait of her daughter, with which he falls instantly in love.

No. 3 Aria TAMINO [8].

This most beautiful of romantic love-songs — a dream of passion, as yet without a real object — is coloured with the warm, amorous tones of clarinets and horns, and set to a vocal line which, alternately soaring in ecstasy and hesitating in doubt and wonder, conveys to perfection Tamino's love-struck state of mind. His growing ardour is reflected not only in the increasingly expressive phrases of the violins (one of them borrowed from *Così fan tutte*) but in the whole form of the aria: at the return of the home key the opening idea does not recur; instead, new and yet more exalted phrases reflect the excited state of Tamino's imagination. Only then is the music of the first section recalled, by the repetition of its concluding phrase, this time expanded into a great arch of soaring melody.

The Three Ladies reappear and, constantly interrupting one another in their excitement, give Tamino the great news. The Queen has heard all; she has chosen him to be the deliverer of her daughter Pamina, kidnapped by a wicked magician and languishing in his castle not far away. Tamino swears to rescue Pamina and begs the Ladies to lead him to the castle at once. At that moment there is a clap of thunder, then two more, and the mountains part to reveal the Queen herself seated on a glittering throne in the midst of a sumptuous palace, surrounded by darkness.

Marcella Sembrich as the Queen of the Night in the Met. première, 1900

No. 4 *Aria* QUEEN OF THE NIGHT.

The imposing orchestral introduction, with insistent violin chords in cross-rhythm over a thrashing bass, suggests a person cast in the heroic mould — and a voice to match: despite the florid runs and dizzy ascents to top F of the aria which follows, the part presupposes not a light coloratura voice but a powerful dramatic soprano with an extended top octave. The music also tells us subtly but unmistakably that the Queen is not what the naive Tamino imagines her to be. Already before the end of the recitative there has been a hint of self-pity as well as self-esteem, and the G minor *Larghetto* [9] confirms it: only contrast the opening phrase — stiffly plaintive, contrived in its pathos — with the similarly shaped but heart-rendingly sincere opening phrase of Pamina's G minor aria in Act Two (No. 17) — example (a).* Half way through, the combination of agitated string accompaniment and long, sinuous bassoon and viola countermelody is reminiscent of Donna Anna's '*Or sai chi l'onore*' in *Don Giovanni* and creates a comparable sensation of suppressed hysteria. The *Allegro* [10], with its brilliantly arrogant flourishes and tense, high horn parts, leaves the same doubts in our minds: this person is not to be taken at face value. As the Queen disappears with a noise of thunder and the mountains close again, Tamino marvels at what he has seen. Was it an illusion? 'Oh kindly gods, do not deceive me! Shield me and strengthen my resolve'. He is about to set out on his quest when Papageno, still padlocked and mumbling pitifully, intercepts him.

No. 5 *Quintet* TAMINO, PAPAGENO, THREE LADIES.

The Quintet begins with a strutting, skipping unison figure on

* Musical Examples (a), (b) and (c) are on page 39.

strings and bassoons, which will be heard again in various forms in the next few scenes, usually in the shape of a trill followed by an arpeggio, and always with a sense of finger-snapping assertiveness — example (b). Papageno, still speechless from the padlock, draws loud attention to his plight, his indignant 'hm's [11] being amusingly combined with Tamino's slightly unctuous expressions of regret at not being able to do anything to help. The Ladies re-appear and remove the padlock. Papageno promises not to tell lies again. After some pious moralising, Tamino is presented with a golden flute which will guard him from harm and bring joy to all who hear it. Papageno is horrified to learn that he is to accompany the Prince on his perilous journey to the castle: Sarastro, the enchanter who rules there, will surely catch him and have him plucked and roasted; but he is placated with the gift of some magic silver bells, which will make men laugh — as the flute will make them love. The two companions bid farewell to the Ladies, who tell them that Three Boys will guide them on their way [12].

The Quintet has the virtuosity of Mozart's most masterly comic ensembles, here refined to a perfection that one would call un-earthly if it were not also so human and alive. Humour and beauty merge into one another, and every incident finds its apt expression within a seemingly effortless musical continuity. The final section, however, in which Tamino and Papageno are told of their young guides, is set slightly apart from the rest of the movement, for it marks the beginning of a new stage in the drama; and at once a strange, mild light, not encountered before, invests the music, as a gentle theme for clarinets and high bassoons floats down above an accompaniment of pizzicato violins. Never was a succession of notes simpler, or more heart-searching. It is a presage of the sublime compassion that we shall experience in the finale of Act Two [33], when the wisdom of the Three Boys guides Pamina on her way.

The fact that the Flute and the Bells, magical agencies of good, are the gifts of the Queen is often cited as evidence for a change in the plot. This is a very literal-minded approach. As we learn later, the Flute is in the possession of the Queen for the reason that it belonged to her late husband, the leader of Sarastro's priesthood, who made it. In any case, magical objects in fairy stories are by tradition morally neutral. As for the Three Boys, to object that they belong to the good side — and therefore should not be in any way associated with, let alone recommended by, the enemy — is to mistake the nature and meaning of the allegory. It is not a question of good versus evil but rather of the progress of the human soul from the darkness of ignorance to the light of understanding, in which state all its former contradictions are reconciled and all its parts, having shed their negative aspects, are united into a single harmonious whole. The Three Ladies represent human develop-ment at its lowest. The strict limitation of their understanding is shown by their inability to do more than set Tamino on the first stage of his quest: they can take him no further, the Boys must replace them. All that is 'inconsistent' about the opening scenes is that in them we see the story from the distorted point of view of the Queen and her creatures. To them Sarastro is an enchanter; the change he works in men seems to the Ladies a mere question of magic. (Similarly the Pamina of the early scenes, being still subject to the influence of her mother the Queen, believes that Papageno will be tortured and killed if Sarastro catches him.) They see the Flute likewise, as a purely magical piece of property, whereas in reality it is a symbol of the power of man and woman united; Tamino and Pamina achieve their goal not by supernatural means but by suffering, self-sacrifice and love.*

In the next scene we are in 'a splendid Egyptian room' in Sarastro's realm. Three slaves excitedly discuss Pamina's escape from the clutches of their master Monostatos. (This part of the work is supposed to have been left over from the original version of the story, in which Monostatos the evil Moor was naturally the servant of the wicked magician; but it is notable that Sarastro is treated sympathetically in the slaves' conversation, in opposition to Monostatos.) A moment later the Moor's angry voice is heard: Pamina has been recaptured, and is dragged in by other slaves at his command.

No. 6 Trio PAMINA, MONOSTATOS, PAPAGENO [13]

A whirlwind *Allegro* in G major. The skipping, finger-snapping figure is much in evidence as Monosatos dances round Pamina. While her phrases from the first show a tendency towards melodic expansion, his are tense and down to earth. His musical idiom is akin to Papageno's but more brutal. He is Papageno's darker self, Natural Man corrupted, enslaved to his selfish appetites and incapable of development (as his name suggests). Throughout the opera his music brilliantly depicts him in a permanent condition of sexual rage and frustration. Yet Papageno, entering the room at the moment when Pamina has fainted and Monostatos is about to satisfy his lust, can without any change of musical style and with only a slight lightening of touch on Mozart's part take over Monostatos's last phrase (in dotted rhythm) and be his own chirpy self. Papageno has just time to comment on the whiteness of Pamina's face (in a musical phrase that exactly echoes a phrase in the G major section of the Ladies' trio, complete with little five-note jingle on the flute — example (c)), before he finds himself face to face with the fearsome Monostatos. The Moor is equally appalled by the apparition of Papageno (whom to the end of the opera he believes to be a huge bird), and each begs the other for mercy, before they both flee in terror. Their brief duet, accompanied by the dotted rhythm in stealthy string octaves, is richly

* See the illuminating essay by Dorothy Koenigsberger, 'A New Metaphor for Mozart's *Magic Flute*', in *European Studies Review*, vol. 5, no. 3, July 1975.

absurd; but some of the humour is lost if their final 'Hu!'s are not sung firmly on the note and sustained to their full length.

Papageno recovers his nerve sooner than Monostatos; and returns just as Pamina regains consciousness. Though they are later to follow very different paths, as befits their different capabilities, the two children of nature make friends at once. Papageno tells Pamina about her mother and the Prince's mission. She needs no portrait to fall instantly in love with Tamino. Papageno glumly reflects that if he cannot find a Papagena he might as well pull all his feathers out. Pamina encourages him to be patient: Heaven will see that his desires are answered, and sooner than he imagines.

No. 7 Duet PAMINA, PAPAGENO [14].

The directness and unsophistication of the melody of this hymn to the power of love, and the plainness of the accompaniment,

'The Magic Flute' at ENO: Valerie Masterson (Pamina) with Alan Opie (Papageno) in the production by Anthony Besch, designed by John Stoddart. (photo: Andrew March)

reflect not only the simplicity of Pamina and Papageno but also their humanity. Although they do not understand what the love they sing about so fervently involves, instinctively Pamina commits herself to it, and Papageno in his more primitive way (his vocal line significantly less abundant and exalted than hers) follows her. The key is E flat major, the Masonic key. They are on the way to achieving the unselfish love between man and woman which is the source of human happiness and by which they may attain divinity. ('Reichen an die Gottheit an').

25

No. 8 Finale.

We return to Tamino, and a crucial moment in the drama. With the first bar, a new sound is heard: a solemn march (*Larghetto*) [15], with soft pulsations of bassoons, trombones and muted trumpets and drums, and the gleam of flutes and clarinets in octaves. Tamino, guided by the Three Boys, has left the domain of Woman. His initiation can begin. Here, the Boys tell him, is his goal, and here, a youth, he must conquer like a man. Will I be able to rescue Pamina, he cries. It is not for them to say. Let him but be steadfast, tolerant, discreet.

Left alone, Tamino looks wonderingly around him. Instead of the frowning walls and embattled turrets of his chivalrous fancies, he sees a pleasant grove, overlooked by three temples inscribed to

David Hockney's design for Act One finale (Glyndebourne, 1978: photo: Guy Gravett)

Nature, Reason and Wisdom — a sanctuary where crime seems to have no place. Very well: he will enter boldly, he has nothing to fear; let the evil-doer tremble, Pamina shall be rescued. Tamino's phrases ring with a fine ardour; but as he advances towards the first of the temples, as though to remind us that he is still confused and ignorant, the violins play the defiant, self-assertive theme (trill followed by arpeggio), which in various forms has been heard several times in the earlier scenes. At the first two temples he is stopped by a voice which cries 'Go back!'. At the third, he knocks on the door and an old priest comes out. Their long dialogue, conducted almost entirely in recitative, is the turning point of the action. If we have understood the allegory of the preceding scenes, the much more elevated tone that now comes over the work is evidence not of any change of intention on the authors' part but rather that the drama has entered a new phase — for which, we can see with hindsight, there have been a number of clear preparatory signs. During their dialogue, under the guidance of the patient, kindly Priest, Tamino takes a decisive step away from ignorance and false values. Yet the ambiguity, the perplexity of his state of mind, is reflected in the fluctuating character of his utterances. At the very beginning, to the Priest's enquiry 'What do you seek in the sanctuary?', he replies like a postulant seeking admission to the rites of initiation, 'The domain of love and virtue', in a serene E flat major with a harmonious accompaniment of clarinets, bassoons and cellos. But that is only a fleeting glimpse of wisdom; Tamino is still breathing fire against Sarastro, and for a long time his phrases have an angry impetuosity, in contrast to the measured calm of the Priest's. (The whole long conversation, with all its weightiness, has a vividness and eloquence that Mozart himself, master of dramatic recitative, never surpassed.) By the end Tamino has come dimly to recognise his error. His aggressiveness has been disarmed; and his final question to the Priest, 'When will the veil be removed?', unconsciously anticipates the moment, now near, when his initiation will begin. The Priest's reply, hopeful but enigmatic, is sung to a noble theme doubled by the cellos. Tamino is left alone: in a desolate A minor, the violins repeat the sad drooping phrase first heard at the point where he had discovered that his enemy Sarastro ruled in the Temple of Wisdom, and all the certainties of his life crumbled to nothing. 'Oh endless night, when will you be gone? When will daylight greet my sight?' He has spoken to himself; but mysterious voices (male), supported by soft trombone chords, answer him from far off, above the Priest's final melody in the cellos, 'Soon, young man, soon or never'. Roused from his dejection, Tamino asks aloud if Pamina still lives. 'Pamina still lives', comes the solemn answer. At that, Tamino in his joy and gratitude to the gods takes out the flute and plays it [16]. At once wild beasts appear, enchanted by its sound. Tamino wonders why it does not also bring Pamina to him; and the music turns to C minor, while oboes memorably add an extra poignancy. He calls Pamina's name; then, when there is no answer, plays a rising scale on the flute. The last five notes are those of Papageno's panpipes, and immediately they answer him from nearby [6]. Tamino's joy overflows, and the music, now an excited *Presto*, flowers into a glorious exaltation: perhaps Papageno has found Pamina and is bringing her to him. He hurries away in search of them.

A moment later the fugitives run in from the opposite side of the stage, to a typically Papageno-like figure in G major [17].(Unlike Tamino, they have not yet learned anything; Papageno, to himself and to Pamina, is still the emissary of the Queen whose task is to rescue Pamina from the evil magician.) A five-note figure prominent in the Quintet is again in evidence; and when Pamina gives expression to her joy in an expansive phrase, the cocky trill-and-arpeggio theme accompanies Papageno's 'Sh, I know better'. He plays his pipes [6]. Tamino's flute answers; and they are hurrying in the direction of the sound when Monostatos creeps up on them (his musical idiom, as before, an angry version of Papageno's), and calls his slaves to tie them up. Just in time Papageno remembers the magic bells, and at their first tinkling strains [18] Monostatos and the slaves are enchanted out of themselves and dance away, laughing with delight. Pamina and Papageno moralise to an exquisite folksong-like tune (echoed later by Schubert's song *Heidenröslein*) [19]. Their moment of happiness is cut short by a fanfare of trumpets and drums, followed by an offstage chorus hailing Sarastro. Both Pamina and Papageno are terrified but the difference in their natures and in their destinies, till now concealed by their common interest and mutual sympathy, is clearly reflected in their music: Papageno's earthy and fragmented, with unison accompaniment, Pamina's expansive and exalted even in fear, and simply but warmly harmonised.

A grand processional chorus in C major now heralds the entry of Sarastro, who arrives in a chariot drawn by six lions. Pamina kneels before him, to five firm chords on strings and woodwind (to which for the first time the gleam of Masonic basset-horns is added). Now more than ever the music conveys the sweetness and nobility of her nature. Her conversation with Sarastro is in a style between arioso and recitative; the musical idiom is without formal restriction of any kind and as natural as speech, yet of unparalleled eloquence. Sarastro (in phrases that Beethoven remembered when he composed the Minister's statement about human brotherhood in the final scene of *Fidelio*) bids Pamina rise, and gently rebukes her, seeking to draw her away from her mother's influence. He knows the secret of her heart. Monostatos has no power over her, she is destined for another, but he cannot yet set her free. Had he left her in her mother's hands, her happiness would have been lost for ever. Only a man can guide her heart's passions to their true fulfilment. Monostatos bustles in (*Allegro*), wheedling and assertive; he has caught Tamino, who with the help of this strange bird (pointing to Papageno) was trying to kidnap Pamina. But Tamino and Pamina have seen one another, and for the moment, in each other's arms, are oblivious of everything else. (It is characteristic of this unconventional work that the lovers' first meeting, should be accomplished almost in parenthesis, in fifteen bars of rapid tempo.) Monostatos drags them apart and, kneeling at Sarastro's feet, demands the reward for faithful service. He is granted it — seventy-seven strokes of the bastinado — and taken away. Sarastro orders Tamino and Papageno to be conducted, with heads covered, to the temple of initiation. The chorus, in jubilant C major with drums and trumpets prominent, sings of virtue and justice, the path to mankind's redemption and the kingdom of heaven upon earth.

Act Two

From now on the work takes on openly the character of a religious initiation, while retaining its *Singspiel* form and pantomime style. Even more than Act One, Act Two is made up of short contrasting scenes; and the trials of Tamino and Pamina are continually offset by the comic adventures of Papageno, as he pursues his destiny on a different level of being, towards his own union of male and female. There are those who are offended by this mixture of high and low; and in an attempt to minimise it, cuts are commonly made in the spoken dialogue. The dialogue, however, contains information necessary for an understanding of the story; and so far from being a weakness and a mere concession to popular taste, the mixture of genres is central to the work. And at every stage of the action the music articulates and illuminates the dramatic situation.

No. 9 March of the Priests [20].

A sacred grove of palm-trees, with silvery trunks and golden leaves symbolising woman and man — the gold superior to the silver (as the sun's direct light is superior to the reflected light of the moon) yet issuing from it. Sarastro and the Priests assemble to the music of a serene, flowing march [20]. For the first time since *Idomeneo*, the spirit of Gluck breathes through Mozart's music. The scoring, full yet lucid, has not been heard in the work before: a single flute, basset-horns, bassoons, horns, trombones and quiet strings.

The Priests take their seats on thrones and, raising golden horns to their lips, blow the Threefold Chord (No. 9a) [1b]. The chord is heard several times during the discussion that follows, in which the Priests listen to and endorse Sarastro's plan for Tamino's initiation and the frustration of the Queen of the Night's plots against the brotherhood. Two priests (one of them known as the Speaker) are sent to bring Tamino and his companion to the temple courtyard and to instruct them in the duties of mankind and the power of the gods.

No. 10 Aria with chorus SARASTRO, PRIESTS [21].

Once again, a completely new sonority — basset-horns, trombones, violas in two parts and cellos (no violins or double basses) — to underline the solemnity of this prayer for the safety of the newly admitted pair in the midst of their perilous ordeals; and, again, music of powerful simplicity. The solo part demands a true bass with strong and resonant low notes and the breath-control to deliver it smoothly, in long phrases, not broken up into groups of a few notes. At the end of each half of the aria, the four-part male chorus repeats the final phrase, with varied distribution of parts — a mysterious effect. The three-bar orchestral epilogue conveys, by the simplest means, a total sense of finality.

A courtyard of the temple. Tamino and Papageno are led in, and the covering is taken from their heads. It is night, and thunder is rumbling. Tamino is steadfast, Papageno panic-stricken. In answer to the Speaker, Tamino promises to undertake the ordeals, but the Second Priest is less successful with his companion, even when he hints that Sarastro may have found him a Papagena who is his living image. Papageno would rather stay single and enjoy his familiar creature comforts than face the ordeals, if he can't have her without them. He promises, however, to remain silent if she appears.

No. 11 Duet TWO PRIESTS [22].

The Second Priest and another (the Speaker's is a non-singing role) emphasise the importance of guarding against the wiles of womankind: death and destruction have overtaken all who disobeyed this cardinal law during the ordeals. The advice is timely, as the next scene will show; yet the old-fashioned, rather pompous cut that Mozart has given their duet — underlined by surprisingly full orchestration (including brass and drums in the final bars) — is surely intentional: Sarastro's plan to include a representative woman in the highest rank of the order is certainly beyond the vision of most of the brotherhood.

On the departure of the priests, the two friends are left alone in the darkness.

No. 12 Quintet THREE LADIES, TAMINO, PAPAGENO [23].

Papageno has time only to cry plaintively for light and Tamino to urge him to be patient, before the Three Ladies spring up out of the earth and confront them: the Queen is near at hand, distressed at their apostasy; they will be destroyed if they give further heed to the lies of the priests and remain a moment longer in the temple. The Ladies' music belies the seriousness of their words. From the first phrase (an echo of the finale of Mozart's string quartet in the same key of G major), it is in the comically frivolous, airy vein of their scenes in Act One. Papageno is nervy and disposed to attend to them but Tamino, prudent and unshakeable, manages to restrain him. The Ladies pout and plead, in vain: they are forced to recognise their failure, and make ready to leave, in music that Mozart is able to make both silly and beautiful. The final G major cadence gives way without warning to a roar of indignation in C minor from an offstage chorus of priests at the profanation of the holy precincts; and to flashes of lightning and thunderclaps and repeated diminished sevenths, fortissimo and across the beat, the Ladies sink into the earth and vanish. Papageno, echoing their final cry of horror, falls to the ground. But the Threefold Chord [1b], ringing out, signals that the ordeal has been passed successfully.

The Speaker and the Second Priest return with torches. Tamino has a hood placed over his head and is led off by the Speaker. The Second Priest with difficulty rouses Papageno and takes him away too, protesting as he goes that this endless trekking about is enough to put a man off love for good.

The scene changes to a garden, with a ring of trees in the shape of a horseshoe, and in the foreground a grassy bank. In the middle of the trees is a rose-arbour, in which Pamina is lying asleep, the moonlight shining on her upturned face. Her ordeals, the equivalent of Tamino's, are about to begin. Monostatos creeps up and observes her hungrily.

No. 13 Aria MONOSTATOS [24].

Monostatos's character as *schwarz*-Papageno is again expressed in this whispered, lustful aria in which the Moor complains angrily of his want of a woman, and resolves to satisfy his hunger with Pamina — if the moon will only hide its light. (Monostatos thus affirms his allegiance to the domain of darkness.) Apart from a single *mezzo forte* accent in each verse, the busy, rapid orchestral accompaniment, topped by piccolo, is *pianissimo* throughout; but Mozart has given it a tingling intensity, comic and diabolical, so that the music positively dances with a kind of Priapic frenzy.

Before Monostatos can touch Pamina, with a clap of thunder the Queen of the Night rises out of the earth beside her couch and dismisses him (he does not go, however, but hides and listens). The conversation between mother and daughter tells us certain important things, in particular of the struggle between matriarchy and patriarchy, passion and reason, which underlies the opera. The Queen's husband, Pamina's father, was Sarastro's predecessor as High Priest of the Sun, and before his death entrusted the emblem of his authority, the seven-fold circle of the sun, not to his wife but to Sarastro. The Queen has been driven to attempt to recover by force what she considers to be rightly hers. Her champion Tamino has been seduced by the enemy and now her daughter too, she urges, is in mortal danger. All will be ended unless Pamina is able to bring Tamino, before dawn illumines the earth, to the subterranean vaults that lead to her domain, or unless, failing that, Pamina kills Sarastro with the dagger that she now thrusts into her hand.

No. 14 Aria QUEEN OF THE NIGHT [25a].

The vengeance of hell boils within her, death and despair flame about her: if Pamina does not plunge the dagger into Sarastro's heart, she is her daughter no longer, she is for ever an outcast. Gods of revenge, hear a mother's oath! The whole style of this prodigious aria, and the orchestration (with its thrillingly decisive interventions of trumpets and drums), suggest a dramatic soprano. Even more than in the Queen's aria in Act One (No. 4), the coloratura [25b] should be sung not lightly but with maximum

31

vehemence; the mask that she wore then is stripped from her. The singer must of course have a range of two octaves, up to top F, but no less necessary is the power to project the manic insistence of those repeated Fs and Gs in the middle of the compass, at 'be rejected for ever, abandoned for ever, destroyed for ever!', and the splendour of the terrifying sustained B flat at the end. The music, adequately sung, is as momentous as the grandest things in *Idomeneo* or *Don Giovanni.*★

Left alone, Pamina rejects the thought of murder. Monostatos reappears and again threatens her. Sarastro intervenes and, dismissing the Moor forever from his service, gently explains to the bewildered girl that she will only find happiness away from her mother. Victory depends on Tamino. If he survives his trials, the Queen will leave the vaults of the temple where now she roams, brooding on revenge, and return to the domain of night, her power finally at an end.

No. 15 Aria SARASTRO [26].

But thoughts of revenge are far from those who dwell in this holy place, where friendship and love are the lights that guide all pilgrims worthy to be called men. The serenity of the aria's flowing melodic lines and the warmth of its flute and bassoon colouring are the positive counterpart of the Queen's outburst of hatred, exorcising its malevolence. As before, Sarastro's music calls for the ample legato and powerful low notes of a true basso cantante.

In another part of the temple, Tamino and Papageno, their heads uncovered, are led in to await their next ordeal. Silence is again enjoined. Tamino has constantly to shush his talkative companion. Papageno longs for a drink. An old hag appears and offers him a large beaker of water. He cannot resist talking to her. When she tells him that she is 18 years old and has a sweetheart called Papageno who is standing right beside her, he throws the water in her face. She is about to tell him her name, when there is a roll of thunder and she vanishes.

No. 16 Trio THREE BOYS [27].

The Three Boys come floating down in an aerial car, bringing the Flute and the Bells and a table laid with food and drink. Their music, in a warm, bright A major full of serene, playful gravity, with whimiscal little flourishes for violins, flutes and bassoons, is as bewitching as any in the score.

Papageno, seemingly uninterested in having the bells restored to him, sets to work on the supper and invites Tamino to join him. Without answering, Tamino takes the flute and plays it. The sound

★ The aria begins, in the voice, with the pattern of notes — D-A-F-E-D — that is found so often in the key of D minor in Mozart's music: e.g., in *Don Giovanni*, 'Fuggi, crudele, fuggi', 'Bisogna aver corraggio' (Act One finale), 'Lascia, lascia alla mia pena' (Sextet). See also the opening of the Piano Concerto K.466 and the Minuet of the Quartet K.421.

brings Pamina running to him but he turns away with a sigh and refuses to speak to her.

No. 17 Aria PAMINA [28].

Pamina gives way to inconsolable grief: never more will her heart know the wonder of love. 'Tamino, see, these tears flow for you alone, beloved. If you feel no answering love, then in death alone will I find peace'. Even by the standards of *The Magic Flute*, the economy and purity of the music are astonishing. The string accompaniment is a simple, almost unvaried succession of short chords in groups of two separated by a rest — a poignant echo of the Act One duet with Papageno (No. 7), where the same pattern of notes in the same metre accompanied her naive declaration of faith in the power of love: here the effect is faltering and piteous. Long-drawn phrases for flute, oboe and bassoon strike sharply across it at moments of harmonic intensification. And the vocal line, in its rise and fall, its keen anguish and utter dejection, is like a musical distillation of suffering itself. After the voice has ceased, the strings, contained till then, well out in a flood of compassion.

The Threefold Chord [1b] now summons Tamino and Papageno. Papageno is in no hurry: he will finish his meal even if Sarastro's lions tried to drag him from it. Immediately the lions appear; and Tamino, hearing his cries, has to hurry back and play the flute to get rid of them. Two further blasts of the Threefold Chord are required before Papageno will join Tamino.

No. 18 Chorus of Priests.

A hall of pyramids. In sonorous D major, with horns, trumpets, and trombones (but no drums) the priests sing a hymn of thanksgiving to the gods [29]. Darkness is in retreat before the brightness of the sun. Tamino is coming into possession of a new life; soon (the word is sung in solemn threefold repetition) he will be an initiate.

Tamino is led in. Sarastro reaffirms the purpose of his mission. Then he calls for Pamina. Amid a profound silence she enters with her head covered. Sarastro removes the covering. He tells her to say goodbye to Tamino.

Emmy Destinn (Pamina), Edward Lankow (Sarastro) and Leo Slezak (Tamino) at the Met.

No. 19 Trio PAMINA, TAMINO, SARASTRO [30].

The music of this hauntingly beautiful piece reflects the ambiguity of the dramatic situation: Pamina and Tamino summoned to bid each other a 'last farewell' yet assured by Sarastro that they will see one another again. The anxious, restless quaver accompaniment on bassoons, violas and cellos is in contrast to the ordered progress of the harmonies and the firm and glowing vocal line of the two men. Pamina sings on her own at first and gives full expression to her feelings in phrase after glorious phrase. Only at Sarastro's words, 'The hour has struck, you must part', do the lovers' voices join, to lament the bitterness of separation and pray for golden peace to fill their hearts. The texture becomes increasingly contrapuntal, the harmonies richer and the emotional expression more passionate, before the quiet, resigned close.*

A moment after they have gone, Papageno runs in, calling for Tamino. Their paths have finally diverged. Papageno tries the doors, only to be driven back each time by a voice crying 'Go back!'. When the Speaker appears and tells him that he will never experience the joys of the initiated, he does not mind, having had more than his fill of the mysteries: there are, as he remarks, plenty of others like him; and he cheers up and forgets his misery when, having told the priest that his greatest and indeed only desire in the world is for a good glass of wine, he sees a great beaker of red wine rise out of the ground. Under its influence he remembers another wish, and plays the magic bells to make it come true.

No. 20 Aria PAPAGENO [31, 32].

A young wife would be bliss for him, he'd be one of the blessed then. If only one of all the lovely girls there are in the world would come to him in his need! If none comes, he'll mope himself to death, he'll burn in his own flame. But a kiss from a little wife would cure everything. The tune is not original to *The Magic Flute*; it was taken from a popular song of the time. The glockenspiel part, increasingly elaborated during the three verses, was played by Mozart at least once, as he described in a letter to his wife Constanze:

> During Papageno's aria with the glockenspiel I went behind the scenes, as I felt a sort of impulse today to play it myself.

* It is sometimes said that this scene makes nonsense of Pamina's subsequent suicide attempt, and that the Trio is wrongly placed and should come earlier. One could reply that such a solution creates more problems than it solves; but the truth is that, except to the literal-minded, there is no problem. The griefs and conflicts under which Pamina will nearly break have not been resolved by the Trio; the crucial question of her mother's influence on her remains to be settled, and her reunion with Tamino has been tantalisingly brief and overshadowed by doubt. Both the music and the words breathe a mood of sadness and poignant tenderness that, for Pamina, is only partly qualified by a vague hope: the most vivid reality is her enforced parting from Tamino. The Trio sounds out of place when performed near the beginning of the act, in a different context from that in which Mozart and Schikaneder placed it.

34

Papageno's aria (No. 20) in the manuscript score

Well, just for fun, at the point where Schikaneder has a pause, I played an arpeggio. He was startled, looked behind the wings and saw me. When he had his next pause, I played no arpeggio. This time he stopped and refused to go on. I guessed what he was thinking and again played a chord. He then struck the glockenspiel [i.e. the magic bells] and said "Shut up". Whereupon everyone laughed. I am inclined to think that this joke taught many of the audience for the first time that Papageno does not play the instrument himself. [*trans.* Emily Anderson]

Papageno's wish is answered instantly, to his alarm, by the reappearance of the old crone, who capers in, leaning on a stick and calling him her angel. Since the alternative, she says, is solitary confinement on bread and water for all eternity, he is forced to swear to be true to her (with reservations). As he does so, she is transformed before his eyes into a young girl with feathers just like himself. He stammers out 'Papagena!' and is on the point of seizing her, when the Speaker whisks her away: Papageno is not yet worthy. As he is vowing to catch her whatever happens to him, the ground gives way beneath him.

No. 21 Finale.

In a small garden, at daybreak, the Three Boys await the rising of the sun which will disperse for ever the dark night of

35

superstition [33]. They pray that peace will enter the hearts of men; then (the words are those of the final chorus of Act One) mankind will achieve the kingdom of heaven on earth. But Pamina still knows no peace. Grief at Tamino's seeming indifference and the final struggle of her soul to free itself from her mother's influence have driven her to the verge of madness, and she has resolved to take her life [34]. The Boys, seeing her wandering about the garden distraught, with the Queen's dagger in her hand, hurry to her and with gentle strength and healing words take charge of her: Tamino loves her and they will lead her to him. Pamina's sorrow is turned to joy. This scene is arguably the loveliest in the score. As in their A major Trio (No. 16), the Boys' music is delicate and airborne, to which the glow of clarinets, bassoons and horns and the key of E flat lend a serene solemnity. The contrast between their flowing, disciplined phrases and Pamina's more and more wild (yet always supremely beautiful) melodic line is marvellously imagined, as is the gradual growth of tension, by means of syncopated upper strings and an increasingly insistent bass, to the moment of truth, where G minor, the key of Pamina's grief, yields decisively to E flat major. Even in the joyful *Allegro* which follows, her line remains wayward at first, as though she can hardly dare to believe what the Boys have told her. Calm returns only gradually to her; when it does, her voice combines with the other three, then breaks free again, to soar up to an exultant high B flat, sustained for four bars, then swooping down nearly two octaves, like a bird released from captivity.

A powerful three-note summons on unison strings and trombones, answered by a plangent phrase for woodwind and cellos, announces the climax of the drama. We are in a harsh landscape, a place where two mountains meet. In one can be seen, through iron grills, a roaring waterfall, in the other a fiery furnace. Between the mountains, a pyramid, with an inscription in transparent letters. Two men in black armour, with flames coming from their helmets, lead in Tamino, lightly dressed and without shoes. They recite the inscription: he who travels this difficult road will be purified by fire, water, air and earth; if he can overcome the terror of death, he will rise to heaven and be received into the mysteries of Isis and Osiris. The music of their chant is a Lutheran chorale ('*Ach Gott, vom Himmel sieh darein*') [35]. Woodwind and trombones play in unison with the two voices, while the strings develop an austere fugue round the chorale, in the manner of Bach [36]. (Mozart had encountered Bach's music, then largely forgotten, at Baron van Swieten's Sunday morning musical gatherings in Vienna, and had also had the opportunity to look through the manuscript parts of some of Bach's motets on his way through Leipzig two years earlier; it may not be mere chance that the rising figure which begins Mozart's fugue subject recalls '*Guter Nacht, o Wesen*' in Bach's motet *Jesu, meine Freude*, where the soul puts the cares and corruptions of worldly life behind it.) The music has generated a formidable tension, and it does not relax when the chorale ends and, to a simple string accompaniment, Tamino steps forward, preparing to enter the gates. The sudden sound of Pamina's voice, calling from near, stops him: 'Tamino, wait — I must see you!' Tamino and the men in armour are shaken out of their solemnity. The music breaks into a surprised and excited *Allegretto*. Now, cries Tamino (and the armed men confirm it), they will never be parted, they will go together into the temple: a woman whom night and death do not frighten is worthy and will be initiated.

The drama has reached its heart. It is now Pamina, refined by suffering, who leads Tamino [37]; and, explaining to him how her father made the Flute, she bids him play it, for its power will carry them through death's dark night. Then they pass into the furnace, and are later seen walking through the waterfall; and when they have passed through, they embrace. A door opens into a temple, brilliantly lit. Pamina and Tamino, 'the noble pair', enter and are welcomed by the brotherhood with shouts of triumph. The sublimity of the '*Magic Flute* style' attains its height in this scene. Nothing could be simpler than the harmonisation of Pamina's vocal line, nothing more obvious than the accompaniment of repeated string chords and long horn and woodwind notes over a rising five-note pizzicato figure in the bass; yet the emotional intensity of this music catches at the listener's heart. It moves with an ease that makes it seem totally natural and unpremeditated; yet when, after Pamina has recounted the origin of the Flute, the tonality regains F major and the four voices combine in an exalted quartet [38], we experience a feeling of concord and perfect fulfilment of which there are few parallels in music. After that there is a pause; and then, as Pamina and Tamino pass through the fire and the water, comes the strangest thing in the score, a climax of mysterious stillness. Without raising his voice, and by means of a quiet march played by a handful of instruments — a slow but florid melody for solo flute [39], punctuated at the end of each phrase by brass chords followed by soft drumbeats (always on the offbeat) — Mozart creates an overwhelming sense of tension, the ordeals of a lifetime compressed into a few bars.

Two more issues remain to be resolved. Papageno, in his search for Papagena, has come to the little garden where the Three Boys saved Pamina from taking her life. He has brought a rope with him, and he attaches it to the branch of a tree. In the intervals of talking he blows his panpipes [6], hoping for an answering bird-call [40], but when none comes his bouncy, irrepressible G major turns to a woebegone G minor (with harmonies that only half-humorously recall Pamina's aria); and, saying goodbye to the perfidious world, he gets ready to hang himself. The Boys, however, are once more at hand, floating down in their aerial car; and just as their influence healed Pamina's grief, so now (in a musical idiom akin to Papageno's earthier chatter) they excitedly remind him of the magic bells, which the silly fellow in his pre-occupation had forgotten: their sound will bring his girl to him. While Papageno, with gleeful solemnity, plays the bells [41], the Boys fetch Papagena from their car. At first, hardly able to believe their good fortune, the two of them can only stare at each other and stammer the syllables of their names [42]. Then, with violins trilling and bassoons gurgling delightedly, they picture the joys of their life together and the endless line of little Papagenos and Papagenas that the gods in their goodness will bless them with. The orchestration is of marvellous freshness and brilliance. Note too the trill-and-arpeggio figure, now innocent and positive, its aggressiveness fruitfully channelled into the begetting of children. Papageno's quest, too, has reached its appointed end.

As they scamper away, the Queen of the Night, Monostatos and the Three Ladies rise from the ground, bent on a last attempt to overthrow the brotherhood. The music [43], in stealthy string staccatos and tremolos, eerie woodwind chords and close vocal harmony, conveys an effect not so much sinister as dreamlike, unreal. The Queen and her creatures, or rather the base appetites and unredeemed attributes they represent, do not have to be defeated by force but can be cast off in one final spasm, to return to the night of illusion to which they belong, for they are by now only shadows, faint memories of former discords in the unenlightened soul, fading for ever in the splendour of the rising sun. There is an elemental roar, with syncopated string chords, a blare of woodwind and brass in diminished seventh harmony, then the sky clears; the stage becomes one radiant sun, with Sarastro on high and Pamina and Tamino in priestly garments, priests on either side of them, and the Three Boys with flowers in their hands. Sarastro, in triumphant recitative, proclaims the passing of night. Then we hear again the C minor music that introduced the scene with the armed men, now transposed into the relative major, a solemn, brilliant E flat, for a hymn of thanksgiving to Isis and Osiris [44]. There follows a jubilant Allegro [45], celebrating the victory of virtue and justice and the everlasting reign of beauty and wisdom.

Perhaps, after all the commentaries that have been lavished on this marvellous work, the wisest words are those uttered by the Three Boys: 'Schweige still' — 'Keep quiet and listen'. Or, as Dent put it, 'The story of the opera is itself a lesson to those who would understand its music; we must prepare ourselves by silence and meditation, we must pass through the fire and water, before we can enter the temple of wisdom'.

Musical Examples

Musical Examples (a), (b) and (c) to which David Cairns refers in the preceding article.

Example (a)

No. 4

No. 17

Example (b)

No. 1

No. 5

No. 5

No. 6

No. 8

No. 8

No. 8

No. 12

No. 21

Example (c)

No. 1

No. 6

No. 8

40

A Public for Mozart's Last Opera

a review of opinions on 'The Magic Flute',
collected and edited by Nicholas John

Since its opening night, Mozart's last opera has been the centre of controversy. The team of Imperial Kapellmeister and populist actor-manager was odd in the first place, and their choice of subject turned out to be something new for Mozart — though in the conventional *Singspiel* form — and unique for the world. But for his thriftlessness, Schikaneder would have made a fortune from the proceeds. In October 1791, there was a performance of it at the Theater auf der Weiden almost every night and he revived it regularly by popular request over the next ten years. The Viennese success was followed by exceptionally well attended productions all over German-speaking Europe. To establish some reasons for this popularity, we may consider firstly the attraction of the stage spectacle, then the dialogue, serious and comic, and lastly the score.

Everyone can sympathise with Mozart's rueful comment about the prospect of taking his mother-in-law to a performance: 'She will see it but not hear it'. Schikaneder spent lavishly on the first production (and indeed on two subsequent ones) in order to please his audience. The effects are essential to the opera, that is, to the music: many commentators have pointed out, for example, how bare the march through the Trials of Fire and Water would sound outside its dramatic context. This was demonstrated many years later, when the impresario of Her Majesty's Theatre in the Haymarket, Benjamin Lumley, gave, at the singer's request, a single 'Grand Classical Performance' of the opera to mark Jenny Lind's return to the London stage; the result was 'a perfect failure'.

'Could it have been otherwise? Any device to treat a lyrical drama as if it were not a drama, or, in other words, to cheat a theatrical representation of its necessary appliances, so as to evade the "stage", could be nothing but a failure. The great masterpiece of Mozart, without the essential accessories of scenery and action, without the illustrative resources which the composer himself contemplated, was simply rendered dreary and incomprehensible. Where was the well-known "Jenny Lind" crush? The house was comparatively empty. Where was the customary enthusiasm amounting to a mania? The applause was cold and feeble. The singer who had been accustomed to hear those same walls ring with plaudits, could not but feel chilled at the faint and rare echoes of that night, so different from the noisy demonstrations of the previous year. The *Flauto Magico* was accordingly the first and last of these disappointing "grand classical performances", permission for which had been with so much difficulty wrung from Mademoiselle Lind . . .'

The very heavy demands made on the scenic artist are partly due

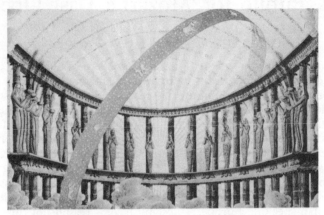

Simon Quaglio's design for Berlin 1816

to the symbolic importance of most of the props and effects. In reply to the enthusiastic recommendation of Frederick William II of Prussia (March 1792), the co-director of the Berlin National Theatre wrote critically,

'It seems to have been the author's intention to crowd together every conceivable difficulty for the stage designer and machinists, and a work has thus been created whose sole merit is visual splendour. At least, it is impossible for an audience which is ignorant of certain mysteries and incapable of seeing through the dark and heavy veil of allegory, to find the slightest interest in it. I regret moreover that the great composer Mozart has had to squander his talent on such unrewarding, mystical and untheatrical material'.

The opera has challenged the imagination of some of the finest theatre designers, notably in our own day Marc Chagall (the Met., 1967) and David Hockney (Glyndebourne, 1978). We are also fortunate that the designs by Schinkel (Berlin, 1816) and Simon Quaglio (Munich, 1818) have been preserved as exquisite examples

Joseph Quaglio's design for Munich 1793

The trials by fire (right) and water (left) in Schikaneder's production, in a coloured engraving by Josef and Peter Schaffer, 1795. Historisches Museum der Stadt Wien)

of neo-classical and early Romantic art. The poet, playwright and composer, E.T.A. Hoffmann, reviewed a performance where Schinkel's designs were used.

'Much has already been said and written about the sets. Suffice it to say that only the so-called *cognoscenti* fail to give due praise to Schinkel's ingenious and subtle creations.

'It was the opinion, in the vicinity of the Reviewer, that the

David Hockney's design for the Trial by Water (Glyndebourne, 1978: photo: Guy Gravett)

moonlight gleaming on the lovely groups of trees in the inner court was entirely natural; to which someone interjected that that was not proper. In his view, the sets should be completely fantastic; for since the characters themselves are not natural, they seem strange and fantastic in a natural setting. He thought it would be a good idea to have red or sky-blue trees. There is an element of truth in this but it is still a fairly strange opinion, from a fairly strange man.'

This articulate approach to *The Magic Flute* leads us to the second controversial element of the opera: just as each of us have a more or less clear personal view about what its fantasy world should look like, we also have decided opinions about how seriously to take Sarastro's pronouncements, and how topical Papageno's jokes should be! The contrast between comedy and solemnity is, in fact, so marked in the dialogue that it lends credit to the claim that it was written by two authors. Giesecke, the actor in Schikaneder's troupe who played the Third Slave and later became Professor of Mineralogy at Dublin University, claimed years later to have written most of it himself, leaving Schikaneder only to write his own comic scenes. We do not know how much Mozart himself contributed to the text. At any rate, subsequent producers have felt free to edit scenes (such as the opening of the second act) and sometimes to omit whole sequences which explain the plot for fear of boring audiences. The result is often no improvement because an audience who cannot understand the action is not in the best position to appreciate the music. The version adopted by ENO recognises this and shortens the scenes without omitting any information necessary to understand the meaning of the opera.

The comic dialogue is very similar to other examples of Viennese *Singspiel*, and Schikaneder himself wrote a sequel (1794) entitled *The Labyrinth or The Struggle for the Elements* in the same vein. (The music was composed by Winter and the project was a failure). Producers have also felt at liberty to update Schikaneder's jokes, so that, for example, Papageno's wine has changed from town to town into a beer from the local brewery. Yet, problematic though the dialogue may be, Mozart's music is unthinkable without it, as anyone who has heard a recording of just the musical numbers will know.

Mozart's score was not, of course, by any means ignored at the time and even Count Zinzendorf (an aristocratic diarist who had no particular sympathy for Mozart's work) noted that the music was 'pretty' — as was the scenery. More importantly, it was greatly admired by Salieri, Mozart's one-time rival for court favour whose musical opinion, after Haydn, he probably valued most, and Madame Cavalieri, the first Constanza in *The Seraglio*. They called it an 'operone' (a grand opera) 'worthy to be performed for the grandest festival and before the greatest monarch'. Another contemporary who took *The Magic Flute* seriously was Goethe, whose mother wrote excitedly to him from Frankfurt about the success of the opera there. (By employing the local children as extras for the animals she noted that even the jobbing gardeners wanted to see the performances!) Goethe himself saw the opera in Weimar in 1795 and the experience inspired him to begin a sequel himself. He never completed *The Magic Flute: Part Two*, possibly because he could not find a composer. It follows the story of Tamino and Pamina's succession to Sarastro, and their parenthood*, and is couched in verse which Einstein found 'full of fairytale radiance, poetic fantasy and profound thought'. Goethe's Tamino, Pamina and the Spirit of their first born child may be seen as models for Faust, Helena and Euphorion in *Faust II*. And in a more far-reaching view, we may trace from the ideals of *The Magic Flute* a recurrent theme of German art — that of a journey, through trials, to enlightenment.

Beethoven revered the ideal (exalted by the French Revolution) of the virtuous love of a man for a woman and enshrined it in *Fidelio*. There are numerous other points of similarity between these operas, notably the brilliant daylight of their triumphant finales, which follow trials in dark prisons. Dent concluded that Beethoven's opera looks back to Mozart more than it looks forward to Weber; and the latter has his own debts to *Die Zauberflöte*. After all, the theme of both *Der Freischütz* and *Euryanthe* is the test of love and fidelity. The fantastic world of *Oberon* is even more familiar because its source is the same book of Oriental tales, the book which was later to furnish Hofmannsthal with the idea for *Die Frau ohne Schatten*.

In these operas, and in *Lohengrin*, *Tannhäuser* and even *Parsifal*, important human spiritual values are expounded in myths and medieval romances. At the core of the fantasy, there is a concern for human virtues, quite distinct from the grand opera popular in France or the Italian *melodramma*.

In a wider sense Liszt and Shaw pointed out that *The Ring Cycle* was *The Magic Flute* of their time. G.B.S. wrote:

'*Die Zauberflöte* is the ancestor, not only of the 9th Symphony but of the Wagnerian allegorical music-drama, with personified abstractions instead of individualised characters as *dramatis personae*'.

---

* The sequence of serious and comic scenes introduces the first-born son of Tamino and Pamina, over whom the other characters of the original struggle for dominance. Sarastro leaves the temple to spend a year in the world of men. The parents' love in the closing scenes assures them of safe passage through the Trials of Fire and Water to see their son, who has been imprisoned in a golden coffin by the Queen of the Night and Monostatos. The boy's spirit greets them and flies up above.

Wagner, himself, acknowledged the greatness of Mozart's music but said,

'It is possible to regret that this great stride of a musical giant should have laid the foundation for German opera and simultaneously imposed its limits by creating the masterpiece of the genre with a sureness of touch that could never be surpassed, and scarcely equalled. Although German opera flourishes today, it is in fact degenerate and declining as fast — alas! — as it reached its peak with Mozart's masterwork'.

To conclude this brief survey of the public reception of Mozart's last opera, let us return to E.T.A. Hoffmann's account of that Berlin performance. Any opera lends itself to disasters in performance and the technical challenge of *The Magic Flute* makes it more vulnerable than most.

Hoffmann refers to the general practice of adding a ballet to the evening's entertainment, which already lasts nearly three hours. One contemporary English critic asked for indulgence from the public for being too tired to stay at opera performances after 1 am!

'*The Magic Flute* has been frequently revived, and always to full houses. This shows how much it repays the trouble of not letting true masterpieces fall into oblivion. Furthermore, although we Germans are accused of always hankering after something new, it is only because we are spoilt by these masterpieces, and so pay no attention to a great deal of newer, poorer stuff, but wait impatiently for something really good to turn up; this is why we are so keen on novelty.

'The performance at the Theatre was excellent as usual, and Mademoiselle Eunike sang the aria '*Ach, ich fühl's*' in particular, in a most affecting manner. The exquisitely beautiful trio '*Soll ich dich Teurer*' was also superbly sung. The acting in the scene in which Papageno and the Moor see each other for the first time, and terrify each other completely, destroyed any intended effect. Where there is exaggeration, art is lost.

'The orchestral playing on this occasion lacked the precision and coherence which usually gives such a fine finish to their performance. The Allegro in the Overture was played too fast, and at the end especially it lost all its clarity. This kind of tempo will do in the concert hall but not in a large theatre, where the sound is muffled.

'A few other passages dragged, in contrast, especially the Chorus exclamation of '*Triumph, Triumph*', which was ragged from start to finish. The main reason for this, however, lies in the practically insurmountable difficulty of having the Chorus perform off-stage. In the libretto, the words 'Unseen Choirs' create a powerful impression but the effect in performance is as poor as the original impression is great. It is more or less

46

essential to find some excuse for bringing the 'Unseen Choirs' into the open, near the orchestra. In the scenes we are speaking of, the Temple Guardians, priests and boys, could appear at each side at the front of the stage (or perhaps better in the front galleries above), while the two purified lovers are being admitted into the Inner Sanctum. The line *'Kommt — kommt'* would be no more out of place than the Spirits' ingenious reply, 'She's out of her mind' (*Sie ist von Sinnen*), to the question 'Where is she then?' (*Wo ist sie denn?*).

' In this context we should not fail to mention the excellent way in which the Spirits played their difficult role. Only once in the Finale of the Second Act were they slightly out of time with each other.

'What a shame it was that the beautiful passage *'Nur stille'* was completely lost due to a fault in the machinery (at least that is what the tree which moved restlessly backwards and forwards seemed to suggest). The Queen and the Moor had already ascended into the Upper World by a different route by the time the Ladies came on, and they had to hurry to greet their mistress with *'Die grosse Königin der Nacht'*.

'The final Chorus went off to perfection, in the most admirable manner. Our Chorus has improved perceptibly thanks to the tireless and praiseworthy efforts of Herr Leidel.

'The close of *The Magic Flute* is grave, solemn, and noble. If there really has to be a Ballet after it, then it should, in the Reviewer's opinion, be either completely unrelated to the opera, or else be performed in the same set, and be closely connected with the thought of the composer, rather than the librettist. The mysteries of Isis and Osiris, such as the consecration, should be represented symbolically, and the dance conceived in the most elevated sense, rather than as a series of amazing leaps and turns. The expressiveness and the novelty of such a performance would soon win over the mass of the public. There would then be no need for the Egyptian god, who was grave to the point of sullenness, or for him to find the comic pair of false Papagenos or the over-jocular Moors in his inner sanctum (his Boudoir), and he would be able to resist the temptation of having them thrown out by his two bronzed acolytes and his guard . . .'

The performance history of the opera outside those German-speaking countries where it was given regularly has been very curious.

In France, the constraints on the Opéra forbidding the presentation of music set to a foreign librettist's text, prompted an arrangement of the libretto under the title *Les Mystères d'Isis* (1801). This not only involved a wholesale reconstruction of the plot and renaming of the characters (Papagena became Mona, for example), but also, for good measure, a total dismemberment of the score. Excerpts from other Mozart operas and Haydn symphonies were included and the whole mixture served up to great public acclaim for several decades. The press dubbed it *Les misères d'ici* and Berlioz recalled (1837),

> 'It was thus, dressed up as an ape, got up grotesquely in cheap finery, with one eye gouged out, an arm withered, a leg broken, that they dared to present the greatest musician in the world to this French public, so delicate, so demanding, saying to it: 'Look — Mozart,' etc. O misérable . . . etc.'

Paris heard a German company in the authentic version in 1827 and waited until 1863 for a French translation.

England first heard the opera (as *Il Flauto magico*) at a benefit night for Giuseppe Naldi, the Italian tenor who had opened to immense success in *Così fan tutte*. It was one of the works presented at Covent Garden in the 1833 German season, when Wilhelmine Schroder-Devrient sang Pamina, the role in which she had made her world debut in 1821 in Vienna. A brilliant cast including Grisi (Pamina), Mario (Tamino), Giorgio Ronconi (Papageno), Karl Formes (Sarastro) and Pauline Viardot-Garcìa (Papagena) sang the opera at Covent Garden in 1851, with a Queen of the Night who reminded the critic Chorley 'of a pea-hen masquerading as a lark'.

Later in the century, Shaw took on Ruskin over his dismissal of the opera in a book on music. The passage is quoted fully because it is a splendid argument in which Shaw admits that his antagonist has 'a hundred times more insight in (his) mistakes than in most other men's accuracies'.

> 'Mr Ruskin is head and ears in love with Music; and so am I; but I am married to her, so to speak, as a professional critic, whereas he is still a wooer, and has the illusions of imperfect knowledge as well as the illuminations of perfect love. Listen to this, for example:
> ' "True music is the natural expression of a lofty passion for a right cause. In proportion to the kingliness and force of any personality, the expression either of its joy or suffering becomes measured, chastened, calm, and capable of interpretation only by the majesty of ordered, beautiful, and worded sound. Exactly in proportion to the degree in which we become narrow in the cause and conception of our passions, incontinent in the utterance of them, feeble of perseverance in them, sullied or shameful in the indulgence of them, their expression by musical means becomes broken, mean, fatuitous, and at last impossible: the measured waves of heaven will not lend themselves to the expression of ultimate vice: it must be for ever sunk in discordance or silence."
> 'I entirely agree with Mr Ruskin in this; but it will not hold

water, for all that. "The measured waves of heaven" are not so particular as he thinks. Music will express any emotion, base or lofty. She is absolutely immoral: we find her in Verdi's last work heightening to the utmost the expression of Falstaff's carnal gloating over a cup of sack, just as willingly as she heightened the expression of "a lofty passion for a right cause" for Beethoven in the Ninth Symphony. She mocked and prostituted the Orpheus legend for Offenbach just as keenly and effectively as she ennobled it for Gluck. Mr Ruskin himself has given an instance of this — a signally wrong instance, by the way; but let that pass for a moment:

' "And yonder musician, who used the greatest power which (in the art he knew) the Father of Spirits ever yet breathed into the clay of this world; who used it, I say, to follow and fit with perfect sound the words of the *Zauberflöte* and of *Don Giovanni* — foolishest and most monstrous of conceivable human words and subjects of thought — for the future amusement of his race! No such spectacle of unconscious (and in that unconsciousness all the more fearful) moral degradation of the highest faculty to the lowest purpose can be found in history".

'This is a capital instance of Mr Ruskin's besetting sin — virtuous indignation. If these two operas are examples of "foolishest and most monstrous" words fitted and followed with perfect sound — that is, with true music — what becomes of the definition which limits true music to "the natural expression of a lofty passion for a right cause"? Clearly, that will not do.

'And now may I beg Mr Ruskin to mend his illustration, if not his argument? The generation which could see nothing in *Die Zauberflöte* but a silly extravaganza was one which Mr Ruskin certainly belonged to in point of time; and he has for once sunk to the average level of its thought in this shallow criticism of the work which Mozart deliberately devoted to the expression of his moral sympathies. Everything that is true and vital in his worship of music would be shattered if it were a fact — happily it is not — that the music of Sarastro came from a silly and trivial mood. If I were to assure Mr Ruskin that Bellini's *Madonna with St Ursula*, in Venice, was originally knocked off as a sign for a tavern by the painter, Mr Ruskin would simply refuse to entertain the story, no matter what the evidence might be, knowing that the thing was eternally impossible. Since he sees no such impossibility in the case of *Die Zauberflöte*, I must conclude that he does not know the masterpieces of music as he knows those of painting.'

To bring the history of performances into this century, we should mention the Cambridge production prepared by E.J. Dent in 1907 and Beecham's performances at Drury Lane in 1914 with the incomparable Claire Dux as Pamina. Richard Tauber sang Tamino for Beecham at Covent Garden in 1938. Sadler's Wells Opera gave it during its first season at the Wells (1931) since when there have been regular revivals of 5 new productions.

'More knowledge is required to understand the value of this libretto than to mock it', wrote Goethe, and the extent of its Masonic significance is only now becoming fully appreciated. There will always be those, like Hoffmann's neighbour, who simply want to establish a fantasy world, with regard for neither realism nor symbolism. Allegory or fairy story? The debate continues. In a review such as this we can only touch upon the variety of attitudes which managements, artists and audiences have expressed towards this great work, in the hope that in future there will be evidence of no less imagination but rather more humility.

A scene from the ENO production, designed by John Stoddart. (photo: Donald Southern)

Thematic Guide

Many of the themes from the opera have been identified in the preceding articles by numbers in square brackets, which refer to the themes on these pages. The original numbers of the musical items in the full score have been noted in italics, and should not be confused with the numbers of the thematic guide. The numbers in square brackets also appear at relevant moments in the libretto so that the words can be related to the musical examples in the thematic guide.

[1a] OVERTURE
Adagio

[1b] THE THREEFOLD CHORD
Adagio

[2]
Allegro

[3] TAMINO (*No. 1 Introduction*)
Allegro

Oh help me! oh help me! can no - bo - dy hear me?
Zu Hil - fe! zu Hil - fe! sonst bin ich ver - lo - ren!

[4] THE THREE LADIES
Allegretto

2nd LADY
I am to
Ich soll - te

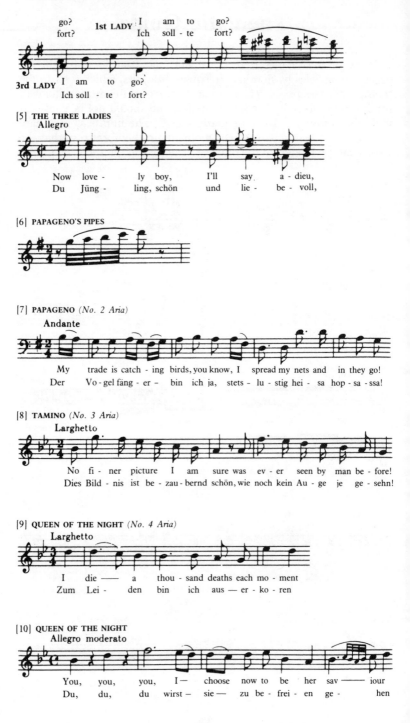

[11] **PAPAGENO** *(No. 5 Quintet)*
Allegro

Hm! hm! hm! hm! hm! hm! hm! hm! hm! hm! hm! hm! hm! hm! hm! hm!

[12] **THE THREE LADIES**
Andante *sotto voce*

Three spir - its, young but old in wis - dom will
Drei Knab - en, jung, schön, hold und wei - se, um -

take you to Sa - ras - tro's king - dom
schwe - ben euch auf eu - rer Rei - se.

[13] **MONOSTATOS, PAMINA** *(No. 6 Trio)*
Allegro molto

M { You won't es - cape, do what you can! P { You are a heart - less e - vil man!
{ Du fei - nes Täub - chen, nur her - ein! { O wel - che Mar. - ter! wel - che Pein!

[14] **PAMINA** *(No. 7 Duet)*
Andantino

The gen - tle love of man and wo - man shows hu - mans
Bei Män - nern, wel - che Lie - be füh - len, fehlt auch - ein

are — a race a - part
gu - tes Her - ze nicht.

[15] **THE THREE BOYS** *(No. 8 Finale)*
Larghetto

The road you trod has led you here, ask here you'll find the goal you're seek - ing.
Zum Zie - le führt dich die - se Bahn, doch musst du, Jüng - ling, männ lich sie - gen.

[16] **THE MAGIC FLUTE**
Andante

53

[17] PAMINA, PAPAGENO
Andante

Walk on tip-toe, cou-rage high. We'll be safe now, you and I.
Schnel-le Füs-se, ra-scher Mut, schützt vor Fein-des List und Wut.

[18] MONOSTATOS'S DANCE
Allegro

[19] PAMINA, PAPAGENO

How I wish that ev'-ry- man
Könn-te jed-er bra-ve Mann

[20] MARCH OF THE PRIESTS (No. 9)
Andante

sotto voce

[21] SARASTRO (No. 10 Aria with Chorus)
Adagio

Oh, Is- is and O- sir- is, hear us, we pray that
O, I- sis und O- si- ris, schen-ket der Weis-heit

you will guide this pair.
Geist dem neu- en Parr!

[22] TWO PRIESTS (No. 11 Duet)
Andante

Be on your guard for wom- man's hu- mours-
Be-wah-ret euch vor Wei- ber- tüc- ken:

[23] THE THREE LADIES (No. 12 Quintet)
Allegro

So! So! So! You are in Sa- ras- tro's court?
Wie? wie? wie? ihr an die-sem Schrec-kens-ort?

54

[24] **MONOSTATOS** (*No. 13 Aria*)

Allegro

pp

All en - joy the beds of pass - ion, cling, ca - ress and stroke and kiss:
Al - les fühlt der Lie - be Freu-den, schnä-belt, tän - delt, herzt und küsst;

[25a] **QUEEN OF THE NIGHT** (*No. 14 Aria*)

Allegro assai

I feel my heart a - flame with hate and mur - der.
Der Höl - le Ra - che kocht in mei - nem Her - zen!

[25b]

Allegro assai

ah ——————————————

[26] **SARASTRO** (*No. 15 Aria*)

Larghetto

To rule by Hate and Ven - geance is not our prac - tice here,
In die - sen heil'gen Hal - len kennt man die Ra - che nicht,

[27] **THE THREE BOYS** (*No. 16 Trio*)

Allegretto

now
Twice we've glad - ly come to meet you
Seid uns zum zwei - ten— mal will-kom-men

[28] **PAMINA** (*No. 17 Aria*)

Andante

Ah, I know that all is end - ed.
Ach, ich fühl's, es ist ver - schwun-den.

[29] **CHORUS** (*No. 18*)

Adagio

p

Oh Is - is and O - sir - is
O Is - is und O - sir - is

[30] **PAMINA, SARASTRO** (*No. 19 Trio*)

Andante moderato

P{ My on - ly joy, ah must we part? S{ You need not fear, but trust his heart.
{ Soll ich dich, Teu - rer, nicht mehr sehn? {Ihr wer - det froh euch wie - der sehn.

[31] **PAPAGENO** (*No. 20 Aria*)
Andante

I'd like a wife to hug me and keep me warm at night.
Ein Mäd - chen o - der Weib - chen wünscht Pa - pa - ge - no sich.

[32] **PAPAGENO**
Allegro

Then liv - ing would give me such plea - sure that
Dann schmeck - te mir Trin - ken und Es - sen, dann

Prin - ces would en - vy my trea - sure
könnt ich mit Für - sten mich mes - sen

[33] **THE THREE BOYS** (*No. 21 Finale*)
Andante

The sun a - ri - ses like a vi - sion and
Bald prangt, den Mor - gen zu ver - kün - den, die

brings a brigh - ter morn;
Sonn' auf gold - ner Bahn.

[34] **PAMINA**
Andante

And so a knife must wed me now?
Du al - so bist mein Bräu - ti - gam!

[35] **THE ARMED MEN**

Man that is born of walks thro' life in sha - dow.
wo - man
Der, wel - cher wan - dert die - se Stra - sse voll Be - schwerd - en,

[36] **FUGUE**
Adagio
p

[37] PAMINA

Andante

Ta - mi - no mine! Oh what great joy!
Ta - mi - no mein! O welch ein Glück!

[38] PAMINA

Andante

We'll walk un - harmed, through mu —
Wir wan — deln durch des To —

TAMINO We'll walk un - harmed thro'
Wir wan - deln durch des

TWO MEN IN ARMOUR They'll walk un - harm — ed
Ihr wan - delt durch — des

— sic's power
— nes Macht

mu sic's power
To - nes Macht

thro' mu - sic's power
To - nes Macht

[39] THE TRIALS MARCH

Adagio

[40] PAPAGENO

Allegro

Pa - pa - ge - na! Pa - pa - ge - na! Pa - pa - ge - na!

[41] PAPAGENO

Allegro

Now bells, let your mu - sic bring my sweetheart here!
Klin - get, Glöck - chen klin - get! schafft mein Mäd - chen her!

57

[42] PAPAGENO, PAPAGENA

[43] MONOSTATOS

[44] CHORUS

[45]

The Magic Flute

an opera in two acts

Libretto by Emanuel Schikaneder
and Carl Ludwig Giesecke
English version: Lyrics by Michael Geliot
Dialogue by Anthony Besch

The complete German text of *Die Zauberflöte* is reprinted here. Although the dialogue is now always shortened in performance, there is no definitive performing edition. Over the years many German variations have been evolved, reflecting changing attitudes to 18th century conventions and what Mozart and his librettists intended or wanted. Whole scenes are sometimes omitted, or re-arranged in sequence; many lines are paraphrased, rewritten or cut. It is very rare for two productions to share the same dialogue.

The English text is the one used by English National Opera at the London Coliseum. Anthony Besch's version of the dialogue (made for his ENO production) is fuller and truer to the original than any previous English version. It is, inevitably, shorter than the German printed here beside it. In order to supply readers with an English rendering of all the original, I have supplied literal translations of passages which are omitted or paraphrased in the performing dialogue. These literal translations form no part whatsoever of the Geliot/Besch performing version and were made only for this Guide. They are clearly distinguished in the text from the performing dialogue by square brackets or, where they were too long to be suitably included in the text, in footnotes.

The stage directions follow Schikaneder's 1791 instructions and do not necessarily reflect the ENO (or any other modern) production. The musical numbers which follow the stage directions after an oblique are those given in the full score. The numbers in square brackets refer to the Thematic Guide.

Authorship of the libretto is traditionally attributed to Giesecke as well as Schikaneder, following E J Dent's monograph (1911) which did much to revive interest in the opera. It is not now accepted by all commentators, *vide* Rodney Milnes. - Editor.

Die Zauberflöte was first performed at the Theater auf der Wieden on September 30, 1791. It was first performed (in Italian) in London at the King's Theatre, Haymarket in 1811 and then at Covent Garden (in German) in 1833. It was first performed in the USA at the Park Theatre, New York, on April 17, 1833.

THE CHARACTERS

Sarastro	bass
Tamino	tenor
The Speaker	bass
A second priest	tenor
An old priest	bass
The Queen of the Night	soprano
Pamina, her daughter	soprano
First ⎫	soprano
Second ⎬ Ladies	soprano
Third ⎭ of the Queen	mezzo-soprano
First ⎫	treble (soprano)
Second ⎬ Boys	treble (soprano)
Third ⎭	alto
Papageno	baritone
Papagena	soprano
Monostatos, a moor	tenor
First ⎫	tenor
Second ⎭ Men in Armour	bass
First ⎫	
Second ⎬ Slaves	speaking parts
Third ⎭	

Priests, Attendants, Populace, Slaves, Voices, Apparitions

Act One

A rocky scene dotted with a few trees. In the centre stands a temple, to which steep paths lead from either side.

Scene One. *Tamino, dressed in a magnificent Japanese hunting costume, enters over one of the rocks: he carries a bow without arrows; he is pursued by a serpent. | Introduction No. 1.*

TAMINO [3]

Oh help me! oh help me! can nobody hear me?	Zu Hilfe! Zu Hilfe! Sonst bin ich verloren,
The venomous fangs of the serpent are near me.	Der listigen Schlange zum Opfer erkoren!
Oh heaven, protect me! I cannot escape.	Barmherziger Götter! Schon nahet sie sich!
Ah rescue me, help me, save me!	Ach rettet mich! Ach schützet mich!

He falls unconscious. At that moment the door of the temple opens and the Three Ladies, veiled, enter each with a silver javelin.

THE THREE LADIES

Now we are here the beast shall die!	Stirb, Ungeheuer, durch unsere Macht!
He dies! He dies! The deed is done,	Triumph! Triumph! Sie ist vollbracht,
The battle won. We've set him free.	Die Heldentat! Er ist befreit
We've saved him through our bravery.	Durch unsres Armes Tapferkeit.

FIRST LADY
(looking at Tamino)

A handsome stranger, full of grace.	Ein holder Jüngling, sanft und schön!

SECOND LADY

I never saw so fair a face.	So schön, als ich noch nie gesehn!

THIRD LADY

Yes, yes, that's true, a lovely face.	Ja, ja, gewiss, zum Malen schön!

THE THREE LADIES

If I should fall in love one day	Würd ich mein Herz der Liebe weihn,
It will be with this youth I pray.	So müsst es dieser Jüngling sein.
But let us hasten to the Queen now	Lasst uns zu unsrer Fürstin eilen,
And tell her what we've done and seen here.	Ihr diese Nachricht zu erteilen.
Perhaps this good man can restore	Vielleicht, dass dieser schöne Mann
The peace and joy she knew before.	Die vor'ge Ruhe ihr geben kann.

FIRST LADY

So hurry and begone,	So geht and sagt es ihr,
I'll guard him here alone.	Ich bleib indessen hier.

SECOND LADY

No, no, I'd rather stay,	Nein, nein, geht ihr nur hin,
I'll watch him thro' the day.	Ich wache hier für ihn!

THIRD LADY

There's no cause for alarm,	Nein, nein, das kann nicht sein,
I'll keep him safe from harm.	Ich schütze ihn allein.

	FIRST LADY
I'll guard him here alone!	Ich bleib indessen hier!

	SECOND LADY
I'll watch him thro' the day!	Ich wache hier für ihn!

	THIRD LADY
I'll keep him safe from harm!	Ich schütze ihn allein!

	FIRST LADY
I'll guard him!	Ich bleibe!

	SECOND LADY
I'll watch him!	Ich wache!

	THIRD LADY
I'll keep him!	Ich schütze!

	ALL THREE
I, I, I.	Ich, ich, ich!

(each one to herself)

I am to go? Oh no, not so.	[4] Ich sollte fort? Ei, ei! Wie fein!
They'd like to be alone	Sie wären gern bei ihm allein.
I know. I shall not go.	Nein, nein, das kann nicht sein.

(one after the other, then all together)

I'd give up all my hopes of heaven	Was wollte ich darum nicht geben,
To live with this young man forever.	Könnt ich mit diesem Jüngling leben!
I know he would be good and kind.	Hätt ich ihn doch so ganz allein!
But they'll not leave, for love is blind!	Doch keine geht, es kann nicht sein.
And so I must be on my way.	Am besten ist es nun, ich geh. —
Now lovely boy, I'll say adieu.	[5] Du Jüngling, schön und liebevoll,
So dear young man, farewell to you.	Du trauter Jüngling, lebe wohl,
We'll meet again I pray.	Bis ich dich wieder seh'!

They go towards the door of the temple, which opens and closes behind them.

TAMINO
(awaking, and looking nervously around)

Where am I? Am I still alive or am I dreaming? The evil serpent lying dead at my feet . . . Have I been protected by Providence?	Wo bin ich? Ist's Phantasie, dass ich noch lebe? Oder hat eine höhere Macht mich gerettet? Wie? — Die bösartige Schlange liegt tot zu meinen Füssen?

He stands up, and looks around. In the distance, panpipes are heard, accompanied quietly by the orchestra. Tamino follows the sound. [6]

What's that I hear? There's a man coming through the trees . . . or something like a man.	Was hör' ich? Wo bin ich? Welch unbekannter Ort? Ha, eine männliche Gestalt nähert sich dem Thale.

He hides behind a tree.

Scene Two. *During the introduction, Papageno comes down a path. On his back he carries a cage of various birds. In his hands he holds the panpipe with which he accompanies his singing. | Aria No. 2*

PAPAGENO [7]

My trade is catching birds, you know,	Der Vogelfänger bin ich ja,
I spread my nets and in they go,	Stets lustig, heissa, hopsassa!

And all men know me as a friend
Throughout the land, from end to end.
I know what ev'ry cockbird likes
So lure the peahen with my pipes.
No wonder that I'm happy then
Since I can catch both cock and hen.

Ich Vogelfänger bin bekannt
Bei alt und jung im ganzen Land.
Weiss mit dem Locken umzugehn
Und mich aufs Pfeifen zu verstehn.
Drum kann ich froh und lustig sein,
Denn alle Vögel sind ja mein.

(He pipes.)

My trade is catching birds, you know,
I spread my nets and in they go,
And all men know me as a friend
Throughout the land, from end to end.
But one thing still I'd like to get
A dozen ladies in my net.
Yes I would think it very fine,
If twelve young maidens could be mine.

Der Vogelfänger bin ich ja,
Stets lustig, heissa, hopsassa!
Ich Vogelfänger bin bekannt
Bei alt und jung im ganzen Land.
Ein Netz für Mädchen möchte ich,
Ich fing sie dutzendweis für mich;
Dann sperrte ich sie bei mir ein,
Und alle Mädchen wären mein.

(He pipes.)

If twelve young maidens could be mine
I'd build a cage of fine design,
I'd choose the one who loved me best,
We'd hop inside and make our nest.
And if she then would be my wife
And kiss and comfort me through life
She'd sleep beside me, snug and warm,
And I would keep her safe from harm.

Wenn alle Mädchen wären mein,
So tauschte ich brav Zucker ein;
Die welche mir am liebsten wär,
Der gäb ich gleich den zucker her.
Und küsste sie mich zärtlich dann,
Wär sie mein Weib und ich ihr Mann.
Sie schlief an meiner Seite ein,
Ich wiegte wie ein Kind sie ein.

He pipes and, when the aria is finished, goes towards the temple door.

TAMINO
(taking him by the hand)

Hey there!   He da!

PAPAGENO

Who's that?   Was da?

TAMINO

You're a lively fellow, my friend . . .
Who are you?

Sag' mir, du lustiger Freund, wer du
bist!

PAPAGENO
(to himself)

That's a silly question —

Wer ich bin? Dumme Frage!

(aloud)

A man like you are. But who are you
anyway?

Ein Mensch, wie du. Wenn ich dich nun
fragte, wer du bist?

TAMINO

Well, to begin with, I'm a prince of royal
blood.

So würde ich dir antworten, dass ich aus
fürstlichem Geblüte bin.

PAPAGENO

Royal blood? Prince? You must speak
more plainly if I'm to understand you.

Das ist mir zu hoch. Musst dich
deutlicher erklären, wenn ich dich
verstehen soll!

TAMINO

My father is a King who rules over many
countries and many people. [That's why
I'm called Prince.]

Mein Vater ist Fürst, der über viele
Länder und Menschen herrscht; darum
nennt man mich Prinz.

63

[Lands? People? Prince?]   Länder? — Menschen? — Prinz?

TAMINO

[That's why I ask you . . .]   Daher frag ich dich —

PAPAGENO

[Slowly! Let me ask the questions!]   Langsam! Lass mich fragen! Sag'
Do you mean to say that beyond these   du mir zuvor: gibt's ausser diesen Bergen
mountains there are other countries and   auch noch Länder und Menschen?
other people?

TAMINO

Yes! Many thousands.   Viele Tausende!

PAPAGENO

What a market for my parakeets.   Da liess' sich eine Spekulation mit
                                                        meinen Vögeln machen.

TAMINO

[Now tell me, in what country are we?]   Nun sag du mir, in welcher Gegend wir
                                                        sind?

PAPAGENO
(looking around)

[In what country? Between valleys and   In welcher Gegend? Zwischen Tälern
mountains.]   und Bergen.

TAMINO

[That's right enough.]   Schon recht. Aber . . .
And now you must tell me who rules this   Wie nennt man eigentlich diese Gegend?
country?   Wer beherrscht sie?

PAPAGENO

How would I know? You might as well   Das kann ich dir ebenso wenig
ask me how I came to be born.   beantworten, als ich weiss, wie ich auf
                                                        die Welt gekommen bin.

TAMINO
(laughing)

Don't you even know who your parents   Wie? Du wüsstest nicht, wo du geboren,
were?   oder wer deine Eltern waren?

PAPAGENO*

I only know that I was brought up by a
strange old man, and that my mother

_____

* This conversation is set out in more detail in the original dialogue as follows:

PAPAGENO

Not a thing! I only know that an old but   Kein Wort! Ich weiss nicht mehr und
very merry man brought me up and fed   nicht weniger, als dass mich ein alter,
me.   aber sehr lustiger Mann auferzogen und
                                                        ernährt hat.

TAMINO

He was your father no doubt!   Das war vermutlich dein Vater?

was once a servant in the temple of the Starblazing Queen. My straw-hut protects me from rain and cold and I earn my living by catching birds for the Queen and her ladies. They give me food and drink in exchange.

TAMINO

Have you ever seen this Starblazing Queen you speak of?

Original dialogue cont'd

PAPAGENO

I don't know.   Das weiss ich nicht.

TAMINO

Did you never know your mother?   Hattest du denn deine Mutter nicht gekannt?

PAPAGENO

I never knew her. I have been sometimes   Gekannt hab ich sie nicht. Erzählen liess
told that my mother used to serve the   ich mir's einigemal, dass meine Mutter
starblazing Queen of the Night. But   einst da in diesem verschlossenen
whether she is still alive or what has   Gebäude bei der nächtlich stern-
become of her, I do not know.   flammenden Königin gedient hätte. Ob
All I do know is that, not far from here,   sie noch lebt oder was aus ihr geworden
is my straw hut which protects me from   ist, weiss ich nicht. Ich weiss nur so viel,
rain and cold.   dass nicht weit von hier meine
                                                Stroh-hütte steht, die mich vor Regen
                                                und Kälte schützt.

TAMINO

But how do you live?   Aber wie lebst du?

PAPAGENO

By eating and drinking, like any other   Von Essen und Trinken, wie alle
man.   Menschen.

TAMINO

How do you obtain that?   Wodurch erhältst du das?

PAPAGENO

From barter. I catch all sorts of birds for   Durch Tausch. Ich fange für die stern-
the starblazing Queen and her ladies; in   flammende Königin und ihre Jungfrauen
exchange I receive daily food and drink   verschiedene Vögel; dafür erhalt ich
from her.   täglich Speis' und Trank von ihr.

TAMINO
(aside)

Starblazing Queen? Supposing it should   Sternflammende Königin? Wenn es etwa
be the powerful sovereign of the night!   gar die mächtige Herrscherin der Nacht
                                                wäre!

(aloud)

Tell me, my good friend, have you ever   Sag mir, guter Freund, warst du schon
been so lucky as to see this goddess of   so glücklich, diese Göttin der Nacht zu
the night?   sehen?

PAPAGENO
(who has been playing his pipes occasionally)

Your last question is so stupid that I can   Deine letzte alberne Frage überzeugt
tell that you come from a different   mich, dass du in einem fremden Land
country.   geboren bist.

65

PAPAGENO

Seen her? You must be crazy! There's no
one alive that's ever seen her. Why are
you staring at me so suspiciously?

TAMINO

Because I'm beginning to doubt whether
you're human.

Weil — weil ich zweifle, ob du Mensch
bist.

PAPAGENO

What's that?

Wie war das?

Original dialogue cont'd

TAMINO

Don't be cross, my good friend! I only
wanted to say —

Sei darüber nicht ungehalten, lieber
Freund! Ich dachte nur —

PAPAGENO

See her? See the starblazing Queen? If
you ask me another such birdbrained
question, as sure as my name is
Papageno I shall pop you in my birdcage
like a bull finch (*pun: 'Gimpel' also means
'birdbrain'*) and sell you with my other
birds to the Queen of the Night and her
ladies. They could then choose, as far as
I'm concerned, between boiling you or
roasting you.

Sehen? Die sternflammende Königin
sehen? Wenn du noch mit einer solchen
albernen Frage an mich kommst, so sperr'
ich dich, so wahr ich Papageno heisse,
wie einen Gimpel in mein Vogel-haus,
verhandle dich dann mit meinen übrigen
Vögeln an die nächtliche Königin und
ihre Jungfrauen; dann mögen sie dich
meinetwegen sieden oder braten.

TAMINO
(aside)

What a strange man!

Ein wunderlicher Mann!

PAPAGENO

See her? See the starblazing Queen?
What mortal could boast of having seen
her? What human sight could see through
her veil woven from darkness?

Sehen? Die sternflammende Königin
sehen? Welcher Sterbliche kann sich
rühmen, sie je gesehen zu haben? Welches
Menschen Auge würde durch ihren
schwarzdurchwebten Schleier blicken
können?

TAMINO

Now it is clear! This must indeed be the
Queen of the Night of whom my father so
often spoke to me. But it is beyond my
comprehension how I can have wandered
here. This man is no ordinary man.
Perhaps he is one of her attendant
spirits.

Nun ist's klar; es ist eben diese
nächtliche Königin, von der mein Vater
mir so oft erzählte. Aber zu fassen,
wie ich mich hierher verirrte, ist ausser
meiner Macht. Unfehlbar ist auch dieser
Mann kein gewöhnlicher Mensch —
vielleicht einer ihrer dienstbaren Geister.

PAPAGENO
(aside)

How he stares at me! I am almost afraid
of him.

Wie er mich so starr anblickt! Bald
fang ich an, mich vor ihm zu fürchten.

(aloud)

Why are you staring at me so
suspiciously?

Warum siehst du so verdächtig und
schelmisch nach mir?

66

Judging by your feathers, you might almost be some kind of bird.

Nach deinen Federn, die dich bedecken, halt' ich dich . . .

PAPAGENO

Don't you insult me! You keep your distance! I'll have you know I've got the strength of a giant.

Doch für keinen Vogel? Bleib zurück, sag' ich, und traue mir nicht; denn ich habe Riesenkraft, wenn ich jemand packe.

(aside)

[If I don't succeed in frightening him, I'll make a hasty exit.]

Wenn er sich nicht bald von mir schrecken lässt, so lauf ich davon.

TAMINO
(He looks at the serpent.)

The strength of a giant? Was it you who rescued me from this serpent?

Riesenkraft? Also warst du wohl gar mein Erretter, der diese giftige Schlange bekämpfte?

PAPAGENO

Serpent? Where?

Schlange? Was da!

(He looks round and suddenly utters a shriek.)

Is it dead or alive?

Ist sie tot oder lebendig?

TAMINO

[You are trying to avoid my thanks with your modest questions.] Thank you for saving my life, I'll always be grateful to you.

Du willst durch deine bescheidene Frage meinen Dank ablehnen. Aber ich muss dir sagen, das ich ewig für deine so tapfere Handlung dankbar sein werde.

PAPAGENO

Think nothing of it — just let's be thankful it's dead.

Schweigen wir davon still. Freuen wir uns, dass sie so glücklich überwunden ist.

TAMINO

But how did you kill it? You have no weapons.

Aber um alles in der Welt, Freund, wie hast du dieses Ungeheuer bekämpft? Du bist ohne Waffen.

PAPAGENO

I don't need them — brute strength.

Brauch keine! Bei mir ist ein starker Druck mit der Hand mehr als Waffen.

TAMINO

You strangled it?

Du hast sie also erdrosselt?

PAPAGENO

Strangled!

Erdrosselt!

(aside)

I've never felt so strong in my life as I do today!

Binin meinem Leben nicht so stark gewesen, als heute.

Enter the Three Ladies.

THE THREE LADIES
(calling threateningly)

Papageno!

Papageno!

PAPAGENO

(That'll be for me.) [Look behind you, friend!]

Aha, das geht mich an! Sieh dich um, Freund!

TAMINO

Who are these ladies?

Wer sind diese Damen?

PAPAGENO

I don't exactly know who they are, but every day I hand over my birds to them and they give me wine, sugar cakes and sweet figs in return.

Wer sie eigentlich sind, weiss ich selbst nicht. Ich weiss nur so viel, dass sie mir täglich meine Vögel abnehmen und mir dafür Wein, Zuckerbrot und süsse Feigen bringen.

TAMINO

Are they very beautiful?

Sie sind vermutlich sehr schön?

PAPAGENO

I shouldn't think so or they wouldn't hide their faces.

Ich denke nicht! Denn wenn sie schön wären, würden sie ihre Gesichter nicht bedecken.

THE THREE LADIES
(menacingly)

Papageno!

Papageno!

PAPAGENO

[Be quiet! Hear how angrily they call me!] Are they beautiful, did you say? I've never seen three such beautiful veiled ladies in my life. (That ought to please them.)

Sei still! Sie drohen mir schon. Du fragst, ob sie schön sind, und ich kann dir darauf nichts antworten, als dass ich in meinem Leben nichts Reizenderes sah. Jetzt werden sie bald wieder gut werden.

THE THREE LADIES

Papageno!

Papageno!

PAPAGENO

(What have I done to make them so angry?) Look, my beauties, here are the birds for your breakfast.

Was muss ich denn heute verbrochen haben, dass sie so aufgebracht wider mich sind? Hier, meine Schönen, übergeb' ich meine Vögel.

FIRST LADY
(handing him a jug of water)

And in return the Queen sends you clear, cold water instead of wine.

Dafür schickt dir unsere Fürstin heute zum ersten Mal statt Wein reines, helles Wasser.

SECOND LADY

And instead of sugar cake she has ordered me to give you this stone. [I hope it does you good.]

Und mir befahl sie, dass ich statt Zuckerbrot diesen Stein dir überbringen soll. Ich wünsche, dass er dir wohl bekommen möge.

PAPAGENO

[What! Must I eat stones?]

Was? Steine soll ich fressen?

THIRD LADY

And instead of ripe figs I have the

Und statt der süssen Feigen hab' ich die

pleasure of closing your mouth with this
golden lock.

Ehre, dir dies goldene Schloss vor den
Mund zu schlagen.

She padlocks his mouth. Papageno protests violently.

FIRST LADY

Do you want to know why the Queen
has punished you today?

Du willst vermutlich wissen, warum die
Fürstin dich heute so wunderbar bestraft?

Papageno nods.

SECOND LADY

So that in future you will not tell lies to
strangers.

Damit du künftig nie mehr Fremde
belügst.

THIRD LADY

And so that you will never again boast of
heroic deeds which were really performed
by others.

Und dass du dich nie der Heldentaten
rühmest, die and're vollzogen.

FIRST LADY

Tell me, did you kill this serpent?

Sag' an, hast du diese Schlange bekämpft?

Papageno shakes his head.

SECOND LADY

Who did then?

Wer denn also?

Papageno shakes his head.

THIRD LADY

It was we *three* who came to your rescue,
young man, but do not be amazed. Joy
and delight await you. Our sovereign
lady the Queen sends you this picture of
her daughter Pamina which I have
painted. If you find that you are not
unmoved by the beauty of this portrait,
then fortune, honour and glory will be
yours. A bientôt, Prince.

Wir waren's Jüngling, die dich befreiten.
Zittre nicht, dich erwartet Freude und
Entzücken. Hier, dies Gemälde schickt
dir die grosse Fürstin; es ist das Bildnis
ihrer Tochter. Findest du, sagte sie, dass
diese Züge dir nicht gleichgültig sind,
dann ist Glück, Ehr' und Ruhm dein
Los! Auf Wiedersehen!

Exit.

SECOND LADY

Adieu, Monsieur Papageno!

Adieu, Monsieur Papageno!

Exit.

THIRD LADY

Don't get indigestion!

Fein nicht zu hastig getrunken!

Exit, laughing.

*Papageno does not stop gesticulating dumbly. Since he received the portrait, Tamino has gazed
at it intently. Deaf to everything he feels his love growing.* **Scene Four** / *Aria No. 3*

TAMINO [8]

No finer picture, I am sure
Was ever seen by man before!

Dies Bildnis ist bezaubernd schön,
Wie noch kein Auge je gesehn!

It moves me, and her pure young face,	Ich fühl es, wie dies Götterbild
Enchants my heart and makes it race.	Mein Herz mit neuer Regung füllt.
This strange and unfamiliar yearning,	Dies Etwas kann ich zwar nicht nennen,
This fierce and ardent pleasure burning —	Doch fühl ich's hier wie Feuer brennen.
What is this sweet and piercing flame?	Soll die Empfindung Liebe sein?
I know! It must be love alone.	Ja, ja! Die Liebe ist's allein.
Oh, how I long to see her glory,	O wenn ich sie nur finden Könnte!
I'd tell her . . . tell her . . . pure and kind . . .	O wenn sie doch schon vor mir stände!
	Ich würde – würde – warm und rein –
What would I say? Upon my heart would I press her,	Was würde ich? – Ich würde sie voll Entzücken
Within these loving arms caress her,	An diesen heissen Busen drücken,
And then I know she would be mine.	Und ewig wäre sie dann mein.

He begins to go.

The Three Ladies return. **Scene Five**

FIRST LADY

Noble youth you must summon up your courage — our Royal Lady . . .	Rüste dich mit Mut und Standhaftigkeit, schöner Jüngling! Die Fürstin . . .

SECOND LADY

Has ordered me to tell you . . .	Hat mir aufgetragen, dir zu sagen . . .

THIRD LADY

That your future happiness is certain. She has . . .	Dass der Weg zu deinem künftigen Glücke nunmehr gebahnt sei.

FIRST LADY

Heard every word you said. She has . . .	Sie hat jedes deiner Worte gehört, so du sprachst; sie hat . . .

SECOND LADY

Read the expression in your face. Her loving mother's heart . . .	Jeden Zug in deinem Gesicht gelesen. Ja noch mehr, ihr mütterliches Herz . . .

THIRD LADY

Has decided to make you really happy. If this youth, she said, is as brave as he is tender-hearted, then my daughter is as good as rescued.	Hat beschlossen, dich ganz glücklich zu machen. Hat dieser Jüngling, sprach sie, auch so viel Mut und Tapferkeit, als er zärtlich ist, o, so ist meine Tochter ganz gewiss gerettet.

TAMINO

Rescued? What do you mean? [Oh endless darkness! The girl in the portrait]	Gerettet? was hör' ich? O ewige Dunkelheit! Das Original –

FIRST LADY

The Princess, Pamina, has been carried off by a powerful and malicious demon.	Wisse, ein böser Dämon hat Paminen ihr entrissen!

TAMINO

[Carried off? O ye Gods! Tell me how this happened.]	Entrissen? O ihr Götter! Sagt, wie konnte das geschehen.

FIRST LADY

One beautiful May morning she was sitting all alone in her favourite cypress grove when the villain sneaked in	Sie sass an einem schönen Maientag ganz allein in dem alles belebenden Zypressenwäldchen, welches immer ihr

un-noticed and stole Pamina away.

Lieblingsaufenthalt war. Der Bösewicht
schlich unbemerkt hinein –

TAMINO

Pamina has been abducted? Where does
the tyrant live?

SECOND LADY

Not far from here in a carefully guarded
fortress.

TAMINO

Show me the way! I will rescue Pamina
and destroy the villain. I swear it by all

Komm't, Mädchen, führ't mich! Sie sei
gerettet. Das schwöre ich bei meiner

---

* The Three Ladies have more to say in the original dialogue.

FIRST LADY (cont'd)

The wicked man sneaked in
unnoticed —

Der Bösewicht schlich unbemerkt
hinein —

SECOND LADY

Spied her —

Belauschte sie und —

THIRD LADY

He has, besides an evil heart, the power
to change into any imaginable shape;
in this way, Pamina was —

Er hat nebst seinem bösen Herzen auch
noch die Macht, sich in jede erdenkliche
Gestalt zu verwandeln; auf solche
Weise hat er auch Pamina —

FIRST LADY

Pamina is the name of the Queen's
daughter, the one whom you adore.

Dies ist der Name der königlichen
Tochter, so Ihr anbetet.

TAMINO

Oh, Pamina! You have been torn away
from me – you are in the power of a
wicked voluptuary! You are perhaps at
this moment – horrible thought –

O Pamina! Du mir entrissen — du in
der Gewalt eines üppigen Bösewichts!
Bist vielleicht in diesem Augenblick —
schrecklicher Gedanke —

THE THREE LADIES

Silence youth!

Schweig, Jüngling!

FIRST LADY

Do not slander the virtue of beauty so
gracious. Innocence bears all patiently,
defiant to torture. Neither force nor
flattery would entice her from the paths
of virtue.

Lästere der holden Schönheit Tugend
nicht. Trotz aller Pein, so die Unschuld
duldet, ist sie sich immer gleich. Weder
Zwang noch Schmeichelei ist vermögend,
sie zum Wege des Lasters zu verführen.

TAMINO

Tell me, ladies, tell me where this tyrant
lives?

O sagt, Mädchen, sagt wo ist des
Tyrannen Aufenthalt?

SECOND LADY

He lives very near to our mountains, in
an enticing and delightful valley. His
impregnable castle is closely guarded.

Sehr nahe an unseren Bergen lebt er in
einem angenehmen und reizenden Tal.
Seine Burg ist prachtvoll und sorgsam
bewacht.

71

I hold sacred.	Leibe, bei meinem Herzen!
	(Thunder)
Heavens, what is that?	Ihr Götter, was ist das?

THE THREE LADIES

Be brave!	Fasse dich!

FIRST LADY

It heralds the arrival of our Queen.	Es verkündet die Ankunft unserer Königin.
	(Thunder)

THE THREE LADIES

She comes! She comes! She comes!	Sie kommt! Sie kommt! Sie kommt!
	(Thunder)

The mountains part and the stage is transformed into a magnificent chamber. **Scene Six.** *The Queen is seated on a throne which gleams with sparkling stars. | Recitative and Aria No. 4*

THE QUEEN

You need not fear, my dearest son,	O zitt're nicht, mein lieber Sohn!
For you are blameless, noble, strong.	Du bist unschuldig, weise, fromm;
A young man like yourself can best imagine	Ein Jüngling, so wie du, vermag am besten
The grief a mother feels, and show compassion.	Dies tiefbetrübte Mutterherz zu trösten.
I die a thousand deaths each moment	[9] Zum Leiden bin ich auserkoren,
Without my daughter by my side,	Denn meine Tochter fehlet mir;
And all my joy is turned to torment —	Durch sie ging all mein Glück verloren,
An evil man took her away.	Ein Bözewicht entfloh mit ihr.
I still see her terror	Noch sehe ich ihr Zittern
When held by her captors,	Mit bangem Erschüttern,
I saw her implore them	Ihr ängstliches Beben,
And tremble before them.	Ihr schüchternes Streben.
I saw the horror all too plainly.	Ich musste sie mir rauben sehen,
'Oh help' I heard her feebly cry.	Ach helft, war alles, was sie sprach;
Alas, I tried but could not save her,	Allein, vergebens ward ihr Flehen,
For all my pow'r was far too weak.	Denn meine Hilfe war zu schwach.
You I choose now to be her saviour,	[10] Du wirst sie zu befreien gehen,
You are the man to set her free.	Du wirst der Tochter Retter sein;
And when you do succeed to save her	Und werd ich dich als Sieger sehen,
I give my word she'll be your bride.	So sei sie dann auf ewig dein.

Exeunt the Queen and Three Ladies. The scene changes back to what it was before. **Scene Seven.**

TAMINO
(after a pause)

Was that vision I saw? [Or are my senses confused?] Oh Gods! Do not deceive me and help me to find Pamina. [Strengthen my arm, uphold my courage, and Tamino's heart will give you eternal thanks.]	Ist's denn auch Wirklichkeit, was ich sah? Oder betäuben mich meine Sinne? O ihr guten Götter, täusch't mich nicht, oder ich unterliege eu'rer Prüfung! Schützet meinen Arm, stählt meinen Mut, und Taminos Herz wird ewigen Dank euch entgegen schlagen.

He begins to leave but Papageno intercepts him. | Quintet No. 5 [11]

(pointing at the padlock on his mouth)

Hm, hm, hm!   Hm, hm, hm!

TAMINO

The poor young man has come to rue it   Der Arme kann von Strafe sagen,
A golden lock has sealed his tongue.   Denn seine Sprache ist dahin.

PAPAGENO

Hm, hm, hm!   Hm, hm, hm!

TAMINO

I'd like to help but can't undo it   Ich kann nichts tun, als dich beklagen,
The magic power is far too strong.   Weil ich zu schwach zu helfen bin.

PAPAGENO

Hm, hm, hm!   Hm, hm, hm!

Scene Eight. *The Three Ladies return.*

FIRST LADY
(taking the lock from Papageno's mouth)

If you will promise you'll repent   Die Königin begnadigt dich,
The Queen will end your punishment.   Erlässt die Strafe dir durch mich.

PAPAGENO

Now hear how Papageno chatters.   Nun plaudert Papageno wieder.

SECOND LADY

But lying is a different matter.   Ja, plaud're! Lüge nur nicht wieder!

PAPAGENO

I'll never tell a lie again!   Ich lüge nimmermehr. Nein! Nein!

THE THREE LADIES

This lock will be your warning then.   Dies Schloss soll deine Warnung sein!

PAPAGENO

The lock shall be my warning then.   Dies Schloss soll meine Warnung sein!

THE THREE LADIES, PAPAGENO

If ev'ry liar were made to wander   Bekämen doch die Lügner alle
With such a lock, for his own good,   Ein solches Schloss vor ihren Mund;
Then hate, destruction, and vile slander   Statt Hass, Verleumdung, schwarzer
                                                        Galle,
Would yield to love and brotherhood.   Bestünde Lieb und Bruderbund.

FIRST LADY
(giving Tamino a golden flute)

Oh Prince, now take this magic flute.   O Prinz, nimm dies Geschenk von mir!
It's given by our Queen's command.   Dies sendet unsre Fürstin dir.
Its pow'r protects thro' ev'ry danger,   Die Zauberflöte wird dich schützen,
In all misfortune it will aid you.   Im grössten Unglück unterstützen.

THE THREE LADIES

You'll rule mankind in godlike fashion,   Hiermit kannst du allmächtig handeln,
It gives power over human passion.   Der Menschen Leidenschaft verwandeln.
It frees the soul of grief and pain   Der Traurige wird freudig sein,

And hardened hearts know love again.   Den Hagestolz nimmt Liebe ein.

ALL

Oh, this holy present is worth far more   O, so eine Flöte ist mehr als Gold und
    than crowns of gold   Kronen wert,
For its power brings human hearts peace   Denn durch sie wird Menschenglück und
    and joy throughout the world.   Zufriedenheit vermehrt.

PAPAGENO

Now you proud and lovely bevy   Nun, ihr schönen Frauenzimmer,
May I take my leave of you?   Darf ich — so empfehl ich mich.

THE THREE LADIES

Papageno, wait a moment.   Dich empfehlen kannst du immer,
Hear the orders of the Queen.   Doch bestimmt die Fürstin dich,
Take the Prince, your task is simple,   Mit dem Prinzen ohn' Verweilen
To Sarastro's secret temple.   Nach Sarastros Burg zu eilen.

PAPAGENO

No, I'm damned if I will go!   Nein, dafür bedank ich mich!
You yourselves have let me know   Von euch selbsten hörte ich,
That he's fiercer than a foe   Dass er wie ein Tigertier!
And, I'm certain, without mercy,   Sicher liess ohn' alle Gnaden
That Sarastro would ill-use me —   Mich Sarastro rupfen, braten,
Chop me, chew me, rip me, pierce me,   Setzte mich den Hunden für.
Then he'd feed me to his dogs.

THE THREE LADIES

Then trust the Prince, he'll keep you safe   Dich schützt der Prinz, trau ihm allein!
If you will be his willing slave.   Dafür sollst du sein Diener sein.

PAPAGENO
(to himself)

To trust the Prince would be plain silly.   Dass doch der Prinz beim Teufel wäre!
My life is all I've got,   Mein Leben ist mir lieb;
I know he'd run off, willy-nilly,   Am Ende schleicht, bei meiner Ehre,
And he'd leave me to rot.   Er von mir wie ein Dieb.

FIRST LADY
(giving Papageno the magic bells in a little box)
Now take this present, do not hide.   Hier nimm dies Kleinod, es ist dein.

PAPAGENO

Ay, ay, I wonder what's inside!   Ei, ei! Was mag darinnen sein?

THE THREE LADIES

You'll find a chime of bells a-ringing.   Darinnen hörst du Glöckchen tönen.

PAPAGENO

And may I also set them swinging?   Werd ich sie auch wohl spielen können?

THE THREE LADIES

Oh yes, of course, of course you may!   O ganz gewiss! Ja, ja gewiss!

ALL

Bells' enchantment, flute's perfection,   Silberglöckchen, Zauberflöten,
They shall be our sure protection.   Sind zu $\left\{ \begin{array}{c} \text{eurem} \\ \text{unserm} \end{array} \right\}$ Schutz vonnöten.

Fare you well, we cannot stay.   Lebet wohl, wir wollen gehn,
So farewell, no more delay.   Lebet wohl, auf Wiedersehn!

74

They all begin to go.

TAMINO

But lovely ladies, good and wise:	Doch schöne Damen, saget an:

PAPAGENO

Tell us which way the temple lies.	Wie man die Burg wohl finden kann?

THE THREE LADIES [12]

Three spirits, young but old in wisdom	Drei Knäblein, jung, schön, hold und weise,
Will take you to Sarastro's kingdom.	Umschweben euch auf eurer Reise;
They'll be your guide in time of need.	Sie werden eure Führer sein,
Take their advice, go where they lead.	Folgt ihrem Rate ganz allein.

TAMINO, PAPAGENO

Three spirits, young, but old in wisdom	Drei Knäblein, jung, schön, hold und weise,
Will take us to Sarastro's kingdom.	Umschweben uns auf unsrer Reise.

ALL

So fare you well, the way is plain.	So lebet wohl! Wir wollen gehn,
Farewell, farewell, we'll meet again.	Lebt wohl, lebt wohl! Auf Wiedersehn!

Exeunt.

Transformation: Scene Nine. *As soon as the scene has changed into a chamber richly furnished in the Egyptian style, two slaves bring on beautiful cushions, and an ornate Turkish table; they roll out carpets. Enter the third slave.*

THIRD SLAVE

Ha, ha, ha!	Hahaha!

SECOND SLAVE

What are you laughing about?	Was soll denn das Lachen?

THIRD SLAVE *

That lascivious Moor, Monostatos, will certainly either be hanged or else beheaded! Pamina has escaped!	

---

* Original dialogue

THIRD SLAVE

Our tormentor, the Moor who overhears all, will certainly be hanged or beheaded tomorrow.	Unser Peiniger, der alles belauschende Mohr, wird morgen sicherlich gehangen oder gespiesst.

FIRST SLAVE

Well?	Nun?

THIRD SLAVE

The delectable maiden! Hahaha!	Das reizende Mädchen! Hahaha!

SECOND SLAVE

Well?	Nun?

THIRD SLAVE

Has escaped.	Ist entsprungen.

FIRST AND SECOND SLAVES

Escaped?	Entsprungen?

SECOND SLAVE

The gods have heard our prayer. For her safety.	O Dank euch, ihr guten Götter! Ihr habt meine Bitte erhört.

FIRST SLAVE

Haven't I always told you that the day of our revenge would come? So Monostatos will be punished for tormenting us and illtreating the girl.	Sagt ich euch nicht immer, es wird doch ein Tag für uns erscheinen, wo wir gerochen und der schwarze Monostatos bestraft werden wird.**

THIRD SLAVE

She was more cunning than I thought and got away under his very eyes.	

FOURTH SLAVE

How was that?	Wieso?

THIRD SLAVE

He tried to rape her but she called out the name of Sarastro. That startled the Moor and he stood as if paralysed. So Pamina ran away to the canal and escaped in a gondola towards the palm grove.	Du kennst ja den üppigen Wanst und seine Weise; das Mädchen aber war klüger, als ich dachte. In dem Augenblick, als er zu siegen glaubte, rief sie Sarastros Namen: das erschütterte den Mohren; er blieb stumm und unbeweglich stehen — indes lief Pamina nach dem Kanal und schiffte von selbst in einer Gondel dem Palmenwäldchen zu.

FIRST SLAVE

[Oh may this timid doe, in mortal terror reach the palace of her beloved mother.]	O wie wird das schüchterne Reh mit Todesangst dem Palast ihrer zärtlichen Mutter zueilen.

Scene Ten. *Monostatos calls from within.*

Footnote cont'd/

FIRST SLAVE

And she got away?	Und sie entkam?

THIRD SLAVE

Certainly. That at least is my dearest wish.	Unfehlbar. Wenigstens ist's mein wahrer Wunsch.

**

SECOND SLAVE

What did the Moor say about this?	Was spricht nun der Mohr zu der Geschichte?

FIRST SLAVE

Has he heard about it yet?	Er weiss doch davon?

THIRD SLAVE

Of course! She escaped right under his nose. According to some of our men, who were working in the garden, and saw and heard everything from a distance, the Moor will not be saved even if Pamina is caught by Sarastro's attendants.	Natürlich! Sie entlief vor seinen Augen. Wie mir einige Brüder erzählten, die in Garten arbeiteten und von weitem sahen und hörten, so ist der Mohr nicht mehr zu retten; auch wenn Pamina von Sarastros Gefolge wieder eingebracht würde.

76

MONOSTATOS

Slaves where are you? Come here to me!   He, Sklaven!

SLAVES

Monostatos!   Monostatos' Stimme!

MONOSTATOS

Bring me chains and fetters!   He, Sklaven! Schafft Fesseln herbei!

SLAVES

[Chains?]   Fesseln?

FIRST SLAVE

[Not for Pamina? Oh ye Gods!]   Doch nicht für Pamina? O ihr Götter!
Look, brothers, the girl has been   Da seht, Brüder, das Mädchen ist
recaptured.   gefangen.

SECOND SLAVE

Pamina! [O wretched sight.]   Pamina! Schrecklicher Anblick!

FIRST SLAVE

The pitiless devil is dragging her back   Seht, wie der unbarmherzige Teufel sie
with him.   bei ihren zarten Händchen fasst – das
[I cannot bear it.]   halt ich nicht aus.

SECOND SLAVE

[Nor I.]   Ich noch weniger.
                    Exit.

THIRD SLAVE

[To have to see this is a hellish torture.]   So was sehen zu müssen, ist
                                              Höllenmarter.
                    Exit.

Slaves drag in Pamina. **Scene Eleven.** / *Trio No. 6*

MONOSTATOS [13]
(very quickly)

You won't escape, do what you can!   Du feines Täubchen, nur herein!

PAMINA

You are heartless evil man!   O welche Marter! Welche Pein!

MONOSTATOS

If life is dear, don't taunt me!   Verloren ist dein Leben!

PAMINA

But Death itself can't daunt me!   Der Tod macht mich nicht beben,
Thoughts of my mother pain me,   Nur meine Mutter dauert mich;
So her grieving heart will break I know. Sie stirbt vor Gram ganz sicherlich.

MONOSTATOS

You slaves, now bind and fetter her.   He, Sklaven! Legt ihr Fesseln an!
I'll teach you to disdain me.   Mein Hass soll dich verderben.

PAMINA

I'd rather you had slain me   O lasst mich lieber sterben,
Than lie here helpless in your power.   Weil nichts, Barbar, dich rühren kann!

She falls senseless on the couch.

MONOSTATOS
(to the slaves)

Now go. Leave me alone with her.

Nun fort! Lasst mich bei ihr allein.

The slaves leave. Papageno appears at the window, at first without being noticed. **Scene Twelve**

PAPAGENO

Where has he gone? I'm on my own?
Aha! there's someone sleeping!
Ah well, I'll go inside —

Wo bin ich wohl? Wo mag ich sein?
Aha, da find ich Leute!
Gewagt, ich geh hinein.

(Enters)

Dear lady, like a bride
You lie there white as powder.

Schön Mädchen, jung und fein,
Viel weisser noch als Kreide!

Papageno notices Monostatos and both are terrified at the sight of each other.

MONOSTATOS, PAPAGENO

Oo! that must – be Lu – cifer – himself!
Have pity! And pardon me!
Oo! Oo! Oo!

Hu! das ist – der Teu – fel si – cherlich!
Hab Mitleid – verschone mich!
Hu! hu! hu!

Both hide. **Scene Thirteen**

PAMINA
(speaking as if in a dream, then recovering herself and looking around)

Mother, mother, mother! Am I still
alive? [Is my heart still not broken?]
Have I woken to new torments? Oh, this
is cruel, more terrible than death.

Mutter — Mutter — Mutter! Wie?
Noch schlägt dieses Herz? Noch nicht
vernichtet? Zu neuen Qualen erwacht?
O, das ist hart, sehr hart — Mir bitterer
als der Tod.

Enter Papageno. **Scene Fourteen**

PAPAGENO

What a fool I was to be so frightened.
There are black birds in the world so
why shouldn't there be black men? The
pretty girl is still there. Greetings,
daughter of the Queen of Night!

Bin ich nicht ein Narr, dass ich mich
schrecken liess? Es gibt ja schwarze
Vögel in der Welt, warum denn nicht
auch schwarze Menschen? Ah, sieh' da!
Hier ist das schöne Fräuleinbild noch.
Du Tochter der nächtlichen Königin!

PAMINA

Who are you?

Wer bist du?

PAPAGENO

A messenger from the Starblazing
Queen.

Ein Abgesandter der sternflammenden
Königin.

PAMINA

From my mother? [Oh joy!] What's your
name?

Meiner Mutter? O Wonne! Dein Name?

PAPAGENO

Papageno.

Papageno.

PAMINA

Papageno? I've often heard of you but

Papageno? Papageno — ich erinnere

never seen you.

mich, den Namen oft gehört zu haben, dich selbst aber sah ich nie.

PAPAGENO

Me neither. I mean I haven't seen you before never neither.

Ich dich ebenso wenig.

PAMINA

So you know my kind and gentle mother?

Du kennst also meine gute, zärtliche Mutter?

PAPAGENO

If you're the daughter of the Nocturnal Monarch, yes! . . . Are you her daughter?

Wenn du die Tochter der nächtlichen Königin bist — ja!

PAMINA

Yes, I am!

O, ich bin es.

PAPAGENO
(taking the portrait given to Tamino which hangs on a ribbon around his neck)

I'll just confirm it . . . Hair dark, dark hair. Eyes black, very black. Lips red, very red. Everything correct except for the hands and feet. According to this picture, you haven't got any.

Das will ich gleich erkennen. Schwarze * Haare — schwarze Haare. Die Augen schwarz — richtig, schwarz. Die Lippen rot – richtig rot. Alles trifft ein, bis auf Hand' und Füsse. Nach dem Gemälde zu schliessen, sollst du weder Hände noch Füsse haben; denn hier sind keine angezeigt.

PAMINA

Let me see. Yes, it's really me. But where did you get it?

Erlaube mir — Ja, ich bin's! Wie kam es in deine Hände?

PAPAGENO †

I'll tell you. This morning I was on my way to your mother's palace to hand over my birds as usual, when I came across a man who calls himself a prince. This prince so impressed your mother that she gave him this picture and ordered him to save you. He fell in love with you and agreed at once.

Eben als ich im Begriffe war, meine Vögel abzugeben, sah ich einen Menschen vor mir, der sich Prinz nennen lässt. Dieser Prinz hat deine Mutter so für sich eingenommen, dass sie ihm dein Bildnis schenkte und ihm befahl, dich zu befreien. Sein Entschluss war so schnell, als seine Liebe zu dir.

---

* Some editions have blond for black hair.
† Original dialogue

PAPAGENO

That's too long a story. It passed from hand to hand.

Dir das zu erzählen, wäre zu weitläufig; es kam von Hand zu Hand.

PAMINA

But how did it come into your hand?

Wie aber in die deinige?

PAPAGENO

In a very curious way. I caught it in a trap.

Auf eine wunderbare Art. Ich hab es gefangen.

PAMINA
(joyfully)

He fell in love with me? Oh, say that again; I like to hear about love.	Liebe? Er liebt mich also? O, sage mir das noch einmal, ich höre das Wort Liebe gar zu gern.

PAPAGENO

I can easily believe that – you're a very sweet young lady. Where was I?	Das glaub' ich dir, ohne zu schwören du bist ja ein Fräuleinbild. Wo blieb ich denn?

PAMINA

Talking about love.	Bei der Liebe.

PAPAGENO

Ah, yes, love. That's what I call a good memory. Well, to make a long story short, his great love for you set us on our way to tell you a thousand nice things, to clasp you in our arms and hurry you back to your mother's palace.	Richtig, bei der Leibe! Das nenn' ich ein Gedächtnis haben! Die grosse Liebe zu dir war der Peitschenstreich, um unsere Füsse in schnellen Gang zu bringen. Nun sind wir hier, dir tausend schöne und angenehme Sachen zu sagen; dich in unsere Arme zu nehmen, und wenn es möglich ist, ebenso schnell, wo nicht schneller als hierher, in den Palast deiner Mutter zu eilen.

PAMINA

That's very nicely said, but if this unknown prince is so much in love with me, why doesn't he come here himself to set me free?	Das ist alles sehr schön gesagt; aber lieber Freund, wenn der unbekannte Jüngling oder Prinz, wie er sich nennt, Liebe für mich fühlt, warum säumt er so lange, mich von meinen Fesseln zu befreien?

PAPAGENO

That's just the problem: when we said goodbye to your mother's three ladies they told us that three spirits would come to show us where to go and how to behave.	Da steckt eben der Haken. Wie wir von den Jungfrauen Abschied nehmen, so sagten sie uns, drei holde Knaben würden unsere Wegweiser sein, sie würden uns belehren, wie und auf welche Art wir handeln sollen.

PAMINA

What did they say?	Sie lehrten euch?

Footnote cont'd

PAMINA

Caught it in a trap?	Gefangen?

PAPAGENO

I had better tell you all the details This morning, as usual, I arrived at your mother's palace to make my delivery . . .	Ich muss dir das umständlicher erzählen. Ich kam heute früh, wie gewöhnlich, zu deiner Mutter Palast mit meiner Lieferung –

PAMINA

Delivery?	Lieferung?

PAPAGENO

Yes. For many years I have delivered to your mother and her ladies all the beautiful birds in the palace.	Ja, ich liefere deiner Mutter und ihren Jungfrauen schon seit vielen Jahren alle die schönen Vögel in den Palast.

80

PAPAGENO

Nothing — we haven't been able to find them yet. So the prince sent me on ahead while he goes on looking for them.	Nichts lehrten sie uns, denn wir haben keinen gesehen. Zu Sicherheit also war der Prinz so fein, mich vorauszuschicken, um dir unsere Ankunft anzukündigen.

PAMINA

You've taken a great risk. If Sarastro should find you . . .	Freund, du hast viel gewagt! Wenn Sarastro dich hier erblicken sollte —

PAPAGENO

Don't suppose I'd be making the return journey?	So würde mir meine Rückreise erspart — das kann ich mir denken.

PAMINA*

There's no time to be lost. We must get away at once.	Wohl denn, es sei gewagt!

(As they leave, Pamina stops.)

But supposing this is a trap and you're a malicious sprite sent by Sarastro?	Aber wenn dies ein Fallstrick wäre – wenn dieser nun ein böser Geist von Sarastros Gefolge wäre?

(She looks at him suspiciously.)

PAPAGENO

Me a malicious sprite? [What are you thinking of?] I'm the nicest sprite in the World.	Ich ein böser Geist? Wo denkst du hin? Ich bin der beste Geist von der Welt.

PAMINA**

[Forgive me, forgive me,] I didn't mean to offend you: I can see that you're really	Vergieb, vergieb, wenn ich dich beleidigte! Du hast ein gefühlvolles Herz;

---

* Original dialogue

PAMINA

You would perish in endless torture.	Dein martervoller Tod würde ohne Grenzen sein.

PAPAGENO

To avoid them, let's leave soon!	Um diesem auszuweichen, gehen wir lieber beizeiten.

PAMINA

What hour is it by the sun?	Wie hoch mag wohl die Sonne sein?

PAPAGENO

It's almost midday.	Bald gegen Mittag.

PAMINA

We must not wait a moment. This is the time when Sarastro usually returns from the hunt.	So haben wir keine Minute zu versäumen. Um diese Zeit kommt Sarastro gewöhnlich von der Jagd zurück.

PAPAGENO

So Sarastro is not at home! Hurray! We've won the game! Come lovely picture Princess. Your eyes will pop out when you catch sight of this handsome young man.	Sarastro ist also nicht zu Hause? Pah, da haben wir gewonnenes Spiel! Komm, schönes Fräuleinbild! Du wirst Augen machen, wenn du denn schönen Jüngling erblickst.

** Original dialogue

PAMINA

Oh, no. The picture convinces me that I am not being tricked. It comes from my good mother's hands.	Doch nein; das Bild hier überzeugt mich, dass ich nicht getäuscht bin; es kommt aus den Händen meiner guten Mutter.

very good-natured [from everything about you.]

das sehe ich in jedem deiner Züge.

PAPAGENO

Of course I'm good-natured, but what's the use of that? I sometimes want to pluck out all my feathers one by one when I remember that Papageno has no Papagena.

Ach, freilich habe ich ein gefühlvolles Herz! Aber was nützt mir das Alles? Ich möchte mir oft alle meine Federn ausrupfen, wenn ich bedenke, dass Papageno noch keine Papagena hat.

PAMINA

Poor man, so you have no wife?

Armer Mann! Du hast also noch kein Weib?

PAPAGENO

Not even a girl-friend, let alone a wife! Yes, it's depressing! Yet even we birdcatchers have time off occasionally when it would be nice to enjoy a few minutes of domestic chat.

Noch nicht einmal ein Mädchen, viel weniger ein Weib! Ja, das ist betrübt! Und unsereiner hat doch auch bisweilen seine lustigen Stunden, wo man gern gesellschaftliche Unterhaltung haben möchte.

PAMINA

Have patience Papageno. The gods will send you a wife sooner than you expect.

Geduld, Freund! Der Himmel wird auch für dich sorgen; er wird dir eine Freundin schicken, ehe du dir's vermutest.

PAPAGENO

If they'd only send her quickly.

Wenn er sie nur bald schickte!

Duet No. 7 [14]

PAMINA

The gentle love of man and woman
Shows humans are a race apart.

Bei Männern, welche Liebe fühlen,
Fehlt auch ein gutes Herze nicht.

PAPAGENO

It is a woman's tender duty
To give a man her loving heart.

Die süssen Triebe mitzufühlen,
Ist dann der Weiber erste Pflicht.

PAMINA, PAPAGENO

While love is ours, we'll freely give;
By love alone we breathe and live.

Wir wollen uns der Liebe freun,
Wir leben durch die Lieb' allein.

PAMINA

It's love that sweetens ev'ry sorrow
And blesses ev'ry waking hour.

Die Lieb' versüsset jede Plage,
Ihr opfert jede Kreatur.

Footnote cont'd

PAPAGENO

Beautiful picture lady, should you have any further wicked doubts, and suspect that I intend to abuse you, you have only to think hard about love and all your dark suspicions will vanish.

Schön's Fräuleinbild, wenn dir wieder ein so böser Verdacht aufsteigen sollte, dass ich dich betrügen wollte, so denke nur fleissig an die Liebe, und jeder böse Argwohn wird schwinden.

82

With love we need not fear the morrow, Sie würzet unsre Lebenstage,
We feel its Universal power. Sie wirkt im Kreise der Natur.

PAMINA, PAPAGENO

We know the goal of human life — Ihr hoher Zweck zeigt deutlich an,
To live in love as man and wife. Nichts Edlers sei, als Weib und Mann.
Wife and man, and man and wife, Mann und Weib und Weib und Mann,
Live in Love, for love is life. Reichen an die Gottheit an.

Both escape. **Transformation.** *The scene changes to a sacred grove. Right at the back is a beautiful temple with the inscription: 'Temple of Wisdom'. Two other temples are joined to this temple by colonnades: the one on the right is inscribed 'Temple of Reason'; the one on the left, 'Temple of Nature'.*
Scene Fifteen. *The Three Boys lead Tamino in, each carrying a silver palm frond. | Finale No. 8*

THE THREE BOYS [15]

The road you trod has led you here, Zum Ziele führt dich diese Bahn,
Ask here, you'll find this goal you're Doch musst du, Jüngling, männlich
  seeking.   siegen.
But you must stand and show no fear. Drum höre unsre Lehre an:
Be constant, patient and be silent. Sei standhaft, duldsam und verschwiegen.

TAMINO

But dear young spirits tell me pray Ihr holden Knaben, sagt mir an,
If my Pamina will be saved. Ob ich Pamina retten kann?

THE THREE BOYS

We may not say: do what you can. Dies kundzutun, steht uns nicht an.
Be constant, patient and be silent. Sei standhaft, duldsam und verschwiegen.
Remember this: you are a man Bedenke dies; kurz, sei ein Mann,
And you will reach the goal you're Dann, Jüngling, wirst du männlich
  seeking.   siegen.

TAMINO

I'll heed their wisdom and I'll cherish Die Weisheitslehre dieser Knaben
Each word of truth until I perish. Sei ewig mir ins Herz gegraben.
Where am I now? How can I tell? Wo bin ich nun? Was wird mit mir?
This seems a place for Gods to dwell. Ist dies der Sitz der Götter hier?
It's written on portals and graven on Es zeigen die Pforten, es zeigen die
  pillars   Säulen,
That Wisdom, Endeavour and Art here Dass Klugheit und Arbeit und Künste
  are rulers,   hier weilen;
Where labour is honoured and idleness Wo Tätigkeit thronet und Müssiggang
  shunned,   weicht,
The hateful corruption of vice can't be Erhält seine Herrschaft das Laster nicht
  found.   leicht.
And so I'll walk thro' each open door. Ich wage mich mutig zur Pforte hinein,
My purpose is worthy and honest and Die Absicht ist edel und lauter und rein.
  fine.
So trembie, cruel sorcerer! Erzitt're, feiger Bösewicht!
To save Pamina is my vow. Pamina retten ist mir Pflicht.

Tamino goes to the righthand door and opens it, but a voice from within declares:

A VOICE

Go back! Zurück!

83

TAMINO

Go back? I'll try here, come what may!   Zurück? So wag ich hier mein Glück!

He approaches the lefthand door, but again a voice proclaims:

A VOICE

Go back!   Zurück!

TAMINO

I'm turned away once more.   Auch hier ruft man: zurück?

(He looks around.)

I see there's yet one more door.   Da seh' ich noch eine Tür,
Perhaps I'll find that way is clear.   Vielleicht find ich den Eingang hier.

He knocks at the central door, it opens and an old priest steps forward.

A PRIEST

Intruder, tell me what you seek.   Wo willst du, kühner Fremdling, hin?
What makes you tread forbidden   Was suchst du hier im Heiligtum?
   ground?

TAMINO

I go where truth and love are found.   Der Lieb' und Tugend Eigentum.

A PRIEST

Those words sound fine and brave, I   Die Worte sind von hohem Sinn!
   know . . .
But say, how do you hope to find them?   Allein, wie willst du diese finden?
For neither love nor truth is found   Dich leitet Lieb' und Tugend nicht,
By men whose hate and vengeance blind   Weil Tod und Rache dich entzünden.
   them.

TAMINO

I only hate the wicked man.   Nur Rache für den Bösewicht.

A PRIEST

You will not find such men within here.   Den wirst du wohl bei uns nicht finden.

TAMINO

Sarastro rules and is your leader.   Sarastro herrscht in diesen Gründen?

A PRIEST

Oh yes, Sarastro rules us here.   Ja, ja! Sarastro herrschet hier!

TAMINO

But not in Wisdom's sacred home?   Doch in dem Weisheitstempel nicht?

A PRIEST

He rules in Wisdom's sacred home.   Er herrscht im Weisheitstempel hier!

TAMINO
(about to leave)

Then it is all deceit and lies.   So ist denn alles Heuchelei!

A PRIEST

So now you wish to go?   Willst du schon wieder gehn?

TAMINO

Yes, I shall go, proud and free,   Ja, ich will gehn, froh und frei,
Far from these temple walls.   Nie euren Tempel sehn.

A PRIEST

Explain your words to me.	Erklär dich näher mir,
I say you are deceived.	Dich täuschet ein Betrug.

TAMINO

Sarastro is your Lord.	Sarastro wohnet hier,
You cannot be believed.	Das ist mir schon genug.

A PRIEST

If you still love your life,	Wenn du dein Leben liebst,
I charge you, stay awhile.	So rede, bleibe da! —
D'you hate Sarastro so?	Sarastro hassest du?

TAMINO

I hate his very name.	Ich hass ihn ewig! Ja!

A PRIEST

At least explain your reasoning.	So gib mir deine Gründe an.

TAMINO

He is inhuman, not a man.	Er ist ein Unmensch, ein Tyrann.

A PRIEST

And have you proof of all you're saying?	Ist das, was du gesagt, erwiesen?

TAMINO

There's proof in that unhappy woman	Durch ein unglücklich Weib bewiesen,
Whose life is filled with bitter tears.	Das Gram und Jammer niederdrückt.

A PRIEST

You take a woman's tears as truth?	Ein Weib hat also dich berückt?
Young man, learn wisdom . . . woman's sighs	Ein Weib tut wenig, plaudert viel.
Are seldom felt and often lies.	Du, Jüngling, glaubst dem Zungenspiel?
Oh, if you know Sarastro well	O, legte doch Sarastro dir
You'd know that ill was not his wish.	Die Absicht seiner Handlung für!

TAMINO

His wishes are as clear as day.	Die Absicht is nur allzu klar;
Did he not steal, without compassion,	Riss nicht der Räuber ohn' Erbarmen
Pamina from her mother's arms?	Pamina aus der Mutter Armen?

A PRIEST

Young man, what you have said is true.	Ja, Jüngling! Was du sagst, ist wahr.

TAMINO

Where is she, she he stole away?	Wo ist sie, die er uns geraubt?
Oh, has her sacrifice begun?	Man opferte vielleicht sie schon?

A PRIEST

I cannot tell you now my son,	Dir dies zu sagen, teurer Sohn,
As yet I'm not allowed to say.	Ist jetzt und mir noch nicht erlaubt.

TAMINO

Explain this myst'ry . . . help me now.	Erklär dies Rätsel, täusch mich nicht.

A PRIEST

An oath of silence is my vow.	Die Zunge bindet Eid und Pflicht.

TAMINO

When shall this secrecy be broken? | Wann also wird die Decke schwinden?

A PRIEST

When friendship offers you its hand | Sobald dich führt der Freundschaft Hand
And bids you join our holy band. | Ins Heiligtum zum ew'gen Band.

The Priest re-enters the Temple.

TAMINO
(to himself)

Oh, endless night, eternal darkness, | O ewige Nacht! Wann wirst du
  | schwinden?
When will the light dispel my blindness? | Wann wird das Licht mein Auge finden?

VOICES
(from within the Temple)

Soon, stranger, you shall see. | Bald, Jüngling, oder nie!

TAMINO

Soon, say if it may be! | Bald, sagt ihr, oder nie?
Mysterious voices, answer me, | Ihr Unsichtbaren, saget mir,
Does my Pamina live? | Lebt denn Pamina noch?

VOICES

Pamina, yes, she lives! | Pamina lebet noch!

TAMINO
(joyfully)

She lives! I need not ask for more. | Sie lebt? Ich danke euch dafür.
Oh, could I find the joyful phrases, | O, wenn ich doch imstande wäre,
Almighty Gods, I'd sing your praises. | Allmächtige, zu eurer Ehre,
This flute shall speak my grateful thanks | Mit jedem Tone meinen Dank
In music; and from here – here it speaks! | Zu schildern, wie er hier, hier entsprang!

Tamino points to his heart. Then he plays on the flute and wild animals and singing birds gather around him. [16]

Ah, now I see your powerful spell, Oh | Wie stark ist nicht dein Zauberton,
  magic flute, —
It is just as strong as I was told | Weil, holde Flöte, durch dein Spielen
Since curious birds and animals come | Selbst wilde Tiere Freude fühlen.
  thronging . . .
Ah, but Pamina does not come. | Doch nur Pamina bleibt davon. —

He plays.

Pamina, hear me. | Pamina! Höre, höre mich!

He plays.

In vain! | Umsonst! —
Where? how can I make you hear? | Wo? Ach, wo find ich dich?

The sound of Tamino's flute is answered by Papageno's pipe. [6]

Ah! That is Papageno's pipe. | Ha, das ist Papagenos Ton!

Papageno again replies on his pipe.

Perhaps he's found Pamina there, | Vielleicht sah er Pamina schon,
Perhaps he's bringing her to me, | Vielleicht eilt sie mit ihm zu mir,
Perhaps, that means my love is near. | Vielleicht führt mich der Ton zu ihr.

Tamino goes off in search of Papageno. Papageno and Pamina enter (without chains). **Scene Thirteen.**

Walk on tip-toe, courage high.   Schnelle Füsse, rascher Mut,
We'll be safe now, you and I.   Schützt vor Feindes List und Wut.
But I hope Tamino's near   Fänden wir Tamino doch,
Or they'll capture us, I fear.   Sonst erwischen sie uns noch!

PAMINA

Oh, Tamino!   Holder Jüngling!

PAPAGENO

Softly, softly, I can lure him.   Stille, stille, ich kann's besser.

He pipes and Tamino's flute is heard in reply.

PAMINA, PAPAGENO

Oh, what joy it is to hear him.   Welche Freude ist wohl grösser?
That's Tamino's flute I know.   Freund Tamino hört uns schon;
Where the flute calls, we must go —   Hierher kam der Flötenton.
Here's an end to care and worry.   Welch ein Glück, wenn ich ihn finde,
Only hurry, only hurry, only hurry!   Nur geschwinde! Nur geschwinde!

Scene Seventeen. *Monostatos surprises them.*

MONOSTATOS

Only hurry, only hurry, only hurry!   Nur geschwinde! Nur geschwinde!
Ha! Now I have caught you both!   Ha, hab ich euch noch erwischt?
I shall clap you both in irons.   Nur herbei mit Stahl und Eisen;
Then I'll feed you to the lions.   Wart, ich will euch Mores weisen.
So you thought that you could cheat me!   Den Monostatos berücken!
It takes more than you to beat me!   Nur herbei mit Band und Stricken,
Ho! You slaves, now bring the ropes.   He, ihr Sklaven, kommt herbei!

Slaves bring chains.

PAMINA, PAPAGENO

Ah! the end of all our hopes.   Ach, nun ist's mit uns vorbei!

PAPAGENO

Do or die, nothing venture, nothing gain.   Wer viel wagt, gewinnt oft viel,
Now, you bells our need is plain,   Komm, du schönes Glockenspiel!
Let me hear your jingle ringle,   Lass die Glöckchen klingen, klingen,
Set their arms and legs a-tingle.   Dass die Ohren ihnen singen.

As Papageno plays the Magic Bells, Monostatos and the Slaves are spell-bound, and begin to dance and sing. [18]

MONOSTATOS, SLAVES

That music enchanting, that music so   Das klinget so herrlich, das klinget so
  pure!   schön!
Larala, larala!   Larala, larala!
I never heard music so fine I am sure.   Nie hab ich so etwas gehört noch gesehn!
Larala, larala!   Larala, larala!

Monostatos and the Slaves dance off.

PAMINA, PAPAGENO [19]

How I wish that ev'ry man   Könnte jeder brave Mann
Could set bells a-ringing,   Solche Glöckchen finden,
Then he'd find that kindness can   Seine Feinde würden dann

Turn all strife to singing.	Ohne Mühe schwinden,
And throughout his life he'd see	Und er lebte ohne sie
Man can live in harmony.	In der besten Harmonie.
Only love and singing,	Nur der Freundschaft Harmonie
Gentle and forgiving,	Mildert die Beschwerden;
Only peace and harmony	Ohne diese Sympathie
Make this life worth living.	Ist kein Glück auf Erden!

The sound of a vigorous march is heard with trumpets and drums.

VOICES
(from within)

All honour Sarastro, Sarastro, hail him!	Es lebe Sarastro, Sarastro lebe!

PAPAGENO

Now what's all this shouting? I'm shiv'ring, I'm quailing.	Wass soll das bedeuten? Ich zittre, ich bebe.

PAMINA

My friend all hope is lost I fear.	O Freund, nun ist's um uns getan!
That sound means that Sarastro's near.	Dies kündigt den Sarastro an.

PAPAGENO

Oh, if I were a mouse,	O, wär ich eine Maus,
I'd vanish down a mousehole!	Wie wollt ich mich verstecken!
Or if I were a tortoise	Wär ich so klein wie Schnecken,
I'd curl up in my house.	So kröch ich in mein Haus.
Oh Lord, deliver us from evil.	Mein Kind, was werden wir nun sprechen?

PAMINA

The Truth will, Truth can shame the devil.	Die Wahrheit, wär sie auch Verbrechen.

Scene Eighteen. *A procession precedes Sarastro, who rides a triumphal chariot, pulled by six lions.*

CHORUS

All honour, Sarastro, Sarastro our leader,	Es lebe Sarastro, Sarastro soll leben!
He rules us with kindness, his service is freedom!	Er ist es, dem wir uns mit Freude ergeben!
Long may he reign over and govern our lives,	Stets mög er des Lebens als Weiser sich freun,
With truth and with justice, all powerful, all wise.	Er ist unser Abgott, dem alle sich weihn.

The chorus continues until Sarastro steps down from his chariot.

PAMINA
(kneeling)

Sir, it is true, I fled from you,	Herr, ich bin zwar Verbrecherin!
And this you well may call a crime.	Ich wollte deiner Macht entfliehn.
But hear, the guilt is not all mine,	Allein die Schuld liegt nicht an mir —
That wicked Moor tried to seduce me	Der böse Mohr verlangte Liebe;
And called it love. I had to fly.	Darum, o Herr, entfloh ich dir.

SARASTRO

Arise and fear no more my dear one.	Steh auf, erheitere dich, o Liebe!
For here we need no inquisition.	Denn ohne erst in dich zu dringen,

88

I know your heart is true and pure.	Weiss ich von deinem Herzen mehr:
You love another that is sure.	Du liebtest einen andern sehr.
I need not curb this true emotion,	Zur Liebe will ich dich nicht zwingen,
Though I can't grant your freedom yet.	Doch geb ich dir die Freiheit nicht.

PAMINA

But there's a voice I can't forget:	Mich rufet ja die Kindes pflicht,
It is my mother's . . .	Denn meine Mutter . . .

SARASTRO

. . . Whom I shall destroy.	. . . Steht in meiner Macht.
Believe me, she would kill your joy	Du würdest um dein Glück gebracht,
If I should yield and hand you over.	Wenn ich dich ihren Händen liesse.

PAMINA

But yet, I still must love my mother	Mir klingt der Muttername süsse;
For she is . . .	Sie ist es . . .

SARASTRO

. . . She is in my pow'r.	. . . Und ein stolzes Weib.
But now a man must guide and teach you.	Ein Mann muss eure Herzen leiten,
For only he turns womankind	Denn ohne ihn pflegt jedes Weib
From paths of pride to ways of virtue.	Aus seinem Wirkungskreis zu schreiten.

Scene Nineteen. *Monostatos brings in Tamino.*

MONOSTATOS

Now, proud young stranger, come this way;	Nun, stolzer Jüngling, nur hierher,
Hear what Sarastro has to say.	Hier ist Sarastro, unser Herr.

PAMINA

Tamino!	Er ist's!

TAMINO

Pamina!	Sie ist's!

PAMINA

I know it's him.	Ich glaub' es kaum!

TAMINO

Pamina!	Sie ist's!

PAMINA

Tamino!	Er ist's!

TAMINO

It must be true.	Es ist kein Traum!

PAMINA

I'll fold you in my arms my dear.	Es schling' mein Arm sich um ihn her!

TAMINO

I'll fold you in my arms my dear.	Es schling' mein Arm sich um sie her!

PAMINA, TAMINO

And though Death come I'll know no fear.	Und wenn es auch mein Ende wär!

They embrace.

What's this intrusion?   Was soll das heissen?

MONOSTATOS
(to Tamino)

What an impertinence,   Welch eine Dreistigkeit!
Release that woman. You go too far.   Gleich auseinander! Das geht zu weit!

(to Sarastro)

Oh Sir, pronounce your fearful sentence.   Dein Sklave liegt zu deinen Füssen,
I bring a sinner to repentance.   Lass den verwegnen Frevler büssen!
Now look upon the evildoer.   Bedenk, wie frech der Knabe ist:
He used this curious birdman's lure   Durch dieses seltnen Vogels List
To steal Pamina from your palace!   Wollt er Pamina dir entführen.
He tried but I have foiled his malice.   Allein ich wusst ihn auszuspüren!
You know me, know my watchful   Du kennst mich! Meine Wachsamkeit —
   eyes . . .

SARASTRO

You've earned the just reward of spies,   Verdient, dass man ihr Lorbeer streut.
So for your service I award . . .   He! Gebt dem Ehrenmann sogleich —

MONOSTATOS

Your kindness overwhelms me, Lord!   Schon deine Gnade macht mich reich.

SARASTRO

Just give him seventy-seven strokes.   — Nur siebenundsiebzig Sohlenstreich.

MONOSTATOS

Oh Lord, I don't know what to say.   Ach, Herr, den Lohn verhofft ich nicht!

SARASTRO

No more, what you have earned, I'll pay.   Nicht Dank, es ist ja meine Pflicht!

Monostatos is taken away.

CHORUS

We honour Sarastro, and all men revere   Es lebe Sarastro, der göttliche Weise!
   him,
He'll punish or pardon — We love him   Er lohnet und strafet in ähnlichem
   and fear him.   Kreise.

SARASTRO

Now lead these two young strangers in   Führt diese beiden Fremdlinge
And thro' our temple be their guide.   In unseren Prüfungstempel ein;
But first ensure their heads are veiled   Bedecket ihre Häupter dann,
For they must now be purified.   Sie müssen erst gereinigt sein.

*The Speaker and the Second Priest each bring a sort of sack which they place over the heads
of the two strangers.*

CHORUS

When justice and integrity   Wenn Tugend und Gerechtigkeit
Fill ev'ry heart with charity,   Den grossen Pfad mit Ruhm bestreut,
When friendship and when brotherhood   Dann ist die Erd' ein Himmelreich,
Teach ev'ry heart to love the good,   Und Sterbliche den Göttern gleich.
Then ev'ry man shall scorn to lie,
The truth shall live and death shall die.

Act Two

The scene is laid in a palm grove. The trees have silvery trunks and golden leaves. There are 18 seats, covered with golden palm leaves, on each of which a pyramid and a large black horn, bound with gold, have been placed. In the centre are the largest pyramid and the tallest palm trees.
Scene One. *Sarastro and the other priests enter solemnly; each holds a palm frond in his hand. A march for wind instruments accompanies them | No. 9 [20]*

SARASTRO

Fellow servants of the great gods Isis and Osiris, hear me! Today's assembly in the Temple of Wisdom is one of the most important we have ever held. Tamino, a king's son, [twenty years of age] is waiting outside the northern gate of our temple. He seeks to achieve the goal which we can only reach through diligence and suffering. He wishes to throw off the veils which one blind him and enter the sanctuary of Light. [It is today one of our most pressing duties to watch over this virtuous man and to offer him the hand of friendship.]

Ihr, in dem Weisheitstempel eingeweihten Diener der grossen Götter Osiris und Isis! Mit reiner Seele erklär' ich euch, dass unsere heutige Versammlung eine der wichtigsten unserer Zeit ist. Tamino, ein Königssohn, zwanzig Jahre seines Alters wandelt an der nördlichen Pforte unseres Tempels und seufzt mit tugendvollem Herzen nach einem Gegenstande, den wir alle mit Mühe und Fleiss erringen müssen. Kurz, dieser Jüngling will seinen nächtlichen Schleier von sich reissen und in's Heiligtum des grössten Lichtes blicken. Diesen Tugendhaften zu bewachen, ihm freundschaftlich die Hand zu bieten sei heute eine unsrer wichtigsten Pflichten.

FIRST PRIEST

Is this man virtuous?

Er besitzt Tugend?

SARASTRO

He is.

Tugend!

SECOND PRIEST

Can he keep silent?

Auch Verschwiegenheit?

SARASTRO

He can.

Verschwiegenheit!

THIRD PRIEST

Is he charitable?

Ist wohltätig?

SARASTRO

Yes. If you consider him worthy, now give the signal.

Wohltätig! – Haltet ihr ihn für würdig, so folgt meinem Beispiele.

First Threefold Chord on the horns | No. 9a

SARASTRO

[Encouraged by the unanimous support of your hearts,] I thank you in the name of humanity. [Prejudice always likes to throw the blame on us, the initiates, but wisdom and reason show up prejudice to be just a spider's web of lies. Prejudice will never shake the pillars of our temple. It will vanish when Tamino has

Menschheit. Mag immer das Vorurteil dankt Sarastro euch im Namen der Menschheit. Mag immer das Vorurteil seinen Tadel über uns Eingeweihte auslassen, Weisheit und Vernunft zerstückt es gleich dem Spinnengewebe. Unsere Säulen erschüttern sie nie. Jedoch das böse Vorurteil soll schwinden, sobald

himself fully mastered the demanding tasks of our art.] The gods have singled out Pamina [the gentle, virtuous maiden] as a bride for Tamino, and for this reason I took her away from her proud mother. That woman [thinks herself powerful. Through deceit and superstition, she hopes to win the people's support and] seeks to destroy our temple but she shall not do so. The noble Tamino shall help us to defend it, [as an initiate,] rewarding virtue and punishing vice.

Tamino selbst die Grösse unserer schweren Kunst besitzen wird. Pamina, das sanfte, tugendhafte Mädchen, haben die Götter dem holden Jünglinge bestimmt; dies ist der Grund, warum ich sie der stolzen Mutter entriss. Das Weib dünkt sich gross zu sein, hofft durch Blendwerk und Aberglauben das Volk zu berücken und unser'n festen Tempelbau zu zerstören. Allein, das soll sie nicht! Tamino, der holde Jüngling selbst, soll ihn mit uns befestigen und als Eingeweihter der Tugend Lohn, dem Laster aber Strafe sein.

Second Threefold Chord

THE SPEAKER
(standing up)

Great Sarastro, we well know and wonder at the wisdom of your words but will Tamino endure the heavy trials which await him? [Forgive me for speaking freely and for expressing my doubts. I am afraid for the young man — that he may, depressed by grief, lose his courage and fall in the difficult fight.] He is a prince.

Grosser Sarastro! deine weisheitsvollen Reden erkennen und bewundern wir; allein, wird Tamino auch die harten Prüfungen, so seiner warten, bekämpfen? Verzeih, dass ich so frei bin, dir meinen Zweifel zu eröffnen! Mir bangt es um den Jüngling. Wenn nun, im Schmerz dahingesunken sein Geist ihn verliesse und er dem harten Kampf unterläge? Er ist Prinz.

SARASTRO

More than that, he is a man.

Noch mehr — er ist Mensch!

THE SPEAKER

What if he should perish in the attempt?

Wenn er nun aber in seiner frühen Jugend leblos erblasste?

SARASTRO

Then he will go to join Isis and Osiris and share their happiness before we do.

Dann ist er Osiris und Isis gegeben, und wird der Götter Freuden früher fühlen, als wir.

Third Threefold Chord

SARASTRO

Send Tamino and his companion into the forecourt of the temple. And you, friends, perform your sacred office and teach them their duty as men.

Man führe Tamino mit seinem Reisegefährten in den Vorhof des Tempels ein.

(to the Speaker who kneels before him)

[And you, my friend, you whom the gods have chosen as the defender of truth, accomplish your sacred duties. May your wisdom instruct the two profane ones in the duties of man and may it teach them the power of the gods.]

Und du, Freund, den die Götter durch uns zum Verteidiger der Wahrheit bestimmten – vollziehe dein heiliges Amt und lehre durch deine Weisheit beide, was Pflicht der Menschheit sei, lehre sie die Macht der Götter erkennen.

Exeunt the Speaker with one of the two priests.

The priests each hold a palm frond and stand around Sarastro. | Aria with chorus No. 10 [21]

SARASTRO

Oh, Isis and Osiris, hear us;	O, Isis und Osiris, schenket
We pray that you will guide this pair.	Der Weisheit Geist dem neuen Paar!
Oh, grant them strength through all temptation,	Die ihr der Wandrer Schritte lenket,
Help them endure all dangers there.	Stärkt mit Geduld sie in Gefahr.

CHORUS

Help them endure all dangers there!	Stärkt mit Geduld sie in Gefahr!

SARASTRO

Should they be worthy then acclaim them,	Lasst sie der Prüfung Früchte sehen;
But if they fail and Death should claim them,	Doch sollten sie zu Grabe gehen,
When for these mortals life shall cease	So lohnt der Tugend kühnen Lauf,
Take them to your abode of peace.	Nehmt sie in euren Wohnsitz auf.

CHORUS

Take them to your abode of peace.	Nehmt sie in euren Wohnsitz auf.

Exit Sarastro, followed by the others.

Transformation. *It is night. Thunder from afar. The scene is a small forecourt of the temple where the remains of sunken columns and pyramids are visible amongst thorn bushes. On both sides stand two high doors in the Egyptian style which represent further buildings at the sides.*
Scene Two. *Tamino and Papageno enter led by the Speaker and the Second Priest, who remove the sacks from their heads and leave them.*

TAMINO

What a fearful night! Papageno, are you still there?	Eine schreckliche Nacht! Papageno, bist du noch bei mir?

PAPAGENO

Yes, more's the pity.	I, freilich!

TAMINO

Where do you think we are?	Wo denkst du, dass wir uns nun befinden?

PAPAGENO

If it wasn't so dark I could see to tell you.	Wo? Ja wenn's nicht finster wäre, wollt' ich dir's sagen – aber so –
	(Thunder)
Oh . . .	O weh! –

TAMINO

What's the matter now?	Was ist's?

PAPAGENO

This spiritual life is so noisy! [*Lit.* I would rather not stick to this subject.]	Mir wird nicht wohl bei der Sache!

TAMINO

You're afraid, it seems to me.	Du hast Furcht, wie ich höre.

PAPAGENO

Certainly not. It's just that there's an ice cold tremor running up and down my spine.	Furcht eben nicht, nur eiskalt läuft's mir über den Rücken. O weh!

	TAMINO
What's happening?	Was soll's?

	PAPAGENO*
I think I must have caught a chill.	Ich glaube, ich bekomme ein kleines Fieber.

Enter The Speaker and Second Priest with torches. **Scene Three.**

	THE SPEAKER
Strangers, what do you seek here? What brings you within our walls?	Ihr Fremdlinge, was such't oder fordert ihr von uns? Was treibt euch an in unsere Mauern zu dringen?

	TAMINO
Friendship and love.	Freundschaft und Liebe.

	THE SPEAKER
Are you ready to fight for them [with your life]?	Bist du bereit, sie mit deinem Leben su erkämpfen?

	TAMINO
Yes.	Ja!

	THE SPEAKER
If necessary with your life?	Auch wenn Tod dein Los wäre?

	TAMINO
Yes.	Ja!

	THE SPEAKER**
Are you willing to undergo every trial?	Du unterzieh'st dich jeder Prüfung?

	TAMINO
I am.	Jeder!

	THE SPEAKER
Your hand.	Reiche mir deine Hand!

The Speaker takes Tamino's hand.

	SECOND PRIEST
[Before you go on, allow me a few words with this other stranger.]	Ehe du weitersprichst, erlaube mir, ein paar Worte mit diesem Fremdling zu sprechen.

---

*Additional dialogue from the original.

	TAMINO
Nonsense, Papageno! Be a man!	Pfui, Papageno! Sei ein Mann!
	PAPAGENO
I would rather be a girl!	Ich wollt', ich wär' ein Mädchen!

(violent thunder clap)

Oh woe! My last hour has come!	O! O! O! Das ist mein letzter Augenblick!

** Additional dialogue from the original.

	THE SPEAKER
Prince, there is still time to withdraw. One more step and it will be too late.	Prinz, noch ist's Zeit zu weichen — einen Schritt weiter, und es ist zu spät.
	TAMINO
May knowledge of wisdom be my achievement and Pamina, the lovely maiden, my reward!	Weisheitslehre sei mein Sieg; Pamina, das holde Mädchen, mein Lohn!

(to Papageno)

And are you ready to fight for the love of wisdom?	Willst auch du dir Weisheitsliebe erkämpfen?

PAPAGENO

Fighting's not my business and I really don't ask for wisdom. I'm [a natural man who's] satisfied with sleep, food and drink — but if I could one day find myself a pretty wife . . .	Kämpfen ist meine Sache nicht. Ich verlange auch im Grund gar keine Weisheit. Ich bin so ein Naturmensch, der sich mit Schlaf, Speise und Trank begnügt; und wenn es ja sein könnte, dass ich mir einmal ein schönes Weibchen fange —

SECOND PRIEST

You'll never find her if you don't undergo our trials.	Die wirst du nie erhalten, wenn du dich nicht unseren Prüfungen unterziehst.

PAPAGENO

But what are these trials?	Worin besteht diese Prüfung?

SECOND PRIEST

To submit to all our laws even if you die in the attempt.	Dich allen unseren Gesetzen zu unterwerfen, selbst den Tod nicht zu scheuen.

PAPAGENO

I'll stay single.	Ich bleibe ledig!

SECOND PRIEST

Even if you could win yourself a virtuous and beautiful wife?	Aber wenn du dir ein tugendhaftes, schönes Mädchen erwerben könntest?

PAPAGENO

I'll stay single.	Ich bleibe ledig.

SECOND PRIEST

But what if Sarastro has a girl waiting for you, and just like you in form and feature?	Wenn nun aber Sarastro dir ein Mädchen aufbewahrt hätte, das an Farbe und Kleidung dir ganz gleich wäre?

PAPAGENO

[Like me?] Is she young?	Mir gleich? — Ist sie jung?

SECOND PRIEST

Young and beautiful.	Jung und schön!

PAPAGENO

What's her name?	Und heisst?

SECOND PRIEST

Papagena.	Papagena.

PAPAGENO

[What? Pa-?]	Wie? Pa-?

SECOND PRIEST

[Papagena!]	Papagena!

PAPAGENO

Papagena? I wouldn't mind seeing her just out of interest.	Papagena? — Die möcht' ich aus blosser Neugierde sehen.

<table>
<tr><td colspan="2" align="center">**SECOND PRIEST**</td></tr>
<tr><td>See her you may . . .</td><td>Sehen kannst du sie! —</td></tr>
</table>

PAPAGENO

But after I've seen her, *then* must I die?	Aber wenn ich sie gesehen habe, hernach muss ich sterben?

Second Priest shrugs his shoulders.

PAPAGENO

I'll stay single.	Ja? — Ich bleibe ledig!

SECOND PRIEST

You can see her but you mustn't speak to her until the appointed time. Do you think you can resist the temptation and hold your tongue?	Sehen kannst du sie, aber bis zur verlauf'nen Zeit kein Wort mit ihr sprechen. Wird dein Geist so viel Standhaftigkeit besitzen, deine Zunge in Schranken zu halten?

PAPAGENO

Of course.	O ja!

SECOND PRIEST

Your hand. You shall see her.	Deine Hand! Du sollst sie sehen.

THE SPEAKER

You too, prince, must remain silent, otherwise you will both perish. You may see Pamina but not speak to her. This silence is commanded as the first of your trials.	Auch dir, Prinz, legen die Götter ein heilsames Stillschweigen auf; ohne dieses seid ihr Beide verloren. – Du wirst Pamina sehen, aber nicht sie sprechen dürfen; dies ist der Anfang eu'rer Prüfungszeit.

Duet No. 11 [22]

THE SPEAKER AND SECOND PRIEST

Be on your guard for woman's humours —	Bewahret euch vor Weibertücken:
That is the rule we follow here.	Dies ist des Bundes erste Pflicht!
For often Man believes her rumours,	Manch weiser Mann liess sich berücken,
She tricks him, and it costs him dear.	Er fehlte und versah sich's nicht.
She promises she'll never hurt him,	Verlassen sah er sich am Ende,
But mocks his heart, that's true and brave;	Vergolten seine Treu mit Hohn!
At last she'll spurn him and deceive him —	Vergebens rang er seine Hände,
Death and despair was all she gave.	Tod und Verzweiflung war sein Lohn.

Exeunt Priests. **Scene Four**

PAPAGENO

Hey, lights there! Lights! [It's odd] Everytime these people go out, the lights go out as well!	He! He! He! Die Lichter her! Die Lichter her!! — Das ist doch sonderbar: so oft einen diese Herren verlassen, so sieht man mit offenen Augen nichts mehr.

TAMINO

Be quiet and remember what they said.	Ertrag es mit Geduld und denke, es ist der Götter Wille.

The Three Ladies suddenly appear. **Scene Five** / *Quintet No. 12* [23]

THE THREE LADIES

So! So! So!	Wie? Wie? Wie?
You are in Sarastro's court?	Ihr an diesem Schreckensort?
Woe! Woe! Woe!	Nie! nie, nie
All your hopes will come to naught!	Kommt ihr wieder glücklich fort!
Tamino, you shall die, you're perjured!	Tamino, dir ist Tod geschworen!
You, Papageno, shall be murdered!	Du, Papageno, bist verloren!

PAPAGENO

No, no, no, I'll die of fright!	Nein, nein, nein! Das wär' zu viel.

TAMINO

Papageno, do be quiet!	Papageno, schweige still!
A promise made cannot be broken,	Willst du dein Gelübde brechen,
But you'll break it once you've spoken.	Nichts mit Weibern hier zu sprechen?

PAPAGENO

You heard that we are both to die.	Du hörst ja, wir sind beide hin.

TAMINO

Just be patient, do be quiet.	Stille, sag ich! Schweige still!

PAPAGENO

Do be quiet and still, be quiet . . .	Immer still und immer still!

THE THREE LADIES

The Queen of Night is now nearby,	Ganz nah ist euch die Königin!
She found a secret way in here.	Sie drang im Tempel heimlich ein?

PAPAGENO

She's what? You say the Queen is near?	Wie? Was? Sie soll im Tempel sein?

TAMINO

Still be silent, quiet I say!	Stille, sag ich! Schweige still!
Must you always chatter,	Wirst du immer so vermessen
Or do promises not matter?	Deiner Eidespflicht vergessen?

THE THREE LADIES

Tamino, you are lost forever,	Tamino, hör! Du bist verloren!
Because you disobey our Queen.	Gedenke an die Königin!
We hear a lot of evil stories	Man zischelt viel sich in die Ohren
About this awful place of sin.	Von dieser Priester falschem Sinn.

TAMINO
(to himself)

The wise man thinks and never fears	Ein Weiser prüft und achtet nicht,
The evil rumours that he hears.	Was der gemeine Pöbel spricht.

THE THREE LADIES

They say that once you join their band,	Man sagt, wer ihrem Bunde schwört,
The Devil drags you down to hell.	Der fährt zur Höll' mit Haut und Haa

PAPAGENO

Now what the Devil, are we damned?	Das wär', beim Teufel, unerhört!
Tell me, Tamino, me as well?	Sag an, Tamino, ist das wahr?

TAMINO

They're only lies old wives repeat,	Geschwätz, von Weibern nachgesagt,
Thought up by those who lie and cheat.	Von Heuchlern aber ausgedacht.

<table>
<tr><td colspan="2" align="center">**PAPAGENO**</td></tr>
<tr><td>They say the Queen is warning you.</td><td>Doch sagt es auch die Königin.</td></tr>
</table>

<table>
<tr><td colspan="2" align="center">**TAMINO**</td></tr>
<tr><td>She's but a fickle woman too.</td><td>Sie ist ein Weib, hat Weibersinn.</td></tr>
<tr><td>Be still, you must believe I'm right;</td><td>Sei still, mein Wort sei dir genug,</td></tr>
<tr><td>Just be a man, and don't take fright.</td><td>Denk deiner Pflicht und handle klug.</td></tr>
</table>

<table>
<tr><td colspan="2" align="center">**THE THREE LADIES**</td></tr>
<tr><td colspan="2" align="center">*(to Tamino)*</td></tr>
<tr><td>Now why do you behave so rudely?</td><td>Warum bist du mit uns so spröde?</td></tr>
<tr><td colspan="2" align="center">*Tamino cautiously indicates that he must not speak.*</td></tr>
<tr><td>You Papageno too — so cruelly?</td><td>Auch Papageno schweigt — so rede!</td></tr>
</table>

<table>
<tr><td colspan="2" align="center">**PAPAGENO**</td></tr>
<tr><td>I'd like to answer that . . .</td><td>Ich möchte gern — wohl —</td></tr>
</table>

<table>
<tr><td colspan="2" align="center">**TAMINO**</td></tr>
<tr><td colspan="2" align="center">*(to Papageno)*</td></tr>
<tr><td>Hush!</td><td>Still!</td></tr>
</table>

<table>
<tr><td colspan="2" align="center">**PAPAGENO**</td></tr>
<tr><td colspan="2" align="center">*(quietly)*</td></tr>
<tr><td>You see I've got to keep . . .</td><td>Ihr seht, dass ich nicht soll. —</td></tr>
</table>

<table>
<tr><td colspan="2" align="center">**TAMINO**</td></tr>
<tr><td>Hush!</td><td>Still!</td></tr>
<tr><td>You find it hard to keep so silent,</td><td>Dass du nicht kannst das Plaudern lassen,</td></tr>
<tr><td>But if you talk you'll get the blame.</td><td>Ist wahrlich eine Schand für dich!</td></tr>
</table>

<table>
<tr><td colspan="2" align="center">**PAPAGENO**</td></tr>
<tr><td>It's really hard to keep so silent,</td><td>Dass ich nicht kann das Plaudern lassen,</td></tr>
<tr><td>But if I talk I'll get the blame.</td><td>Ist wahrlich eine Schand für mich!</td></tr>
</table>

<table>
<tr><td colspan="2" align="center">**THE THREE LADIES**</td></tr>
<tr><td>And now we see they're both defiant</td><td>Wir müssen sie mit Scham verlassen,</td></tr>
<tr><td>We'll have to leave them, full of shame.</td><td>Es plaudert keiner sicherlich;</td></tr>
<tr><td>For Man is silent and he's strong . . .</td><td>Von festem Geiste ist ein Mann,</td></tr>
<tr><td>He knows the time to hold his tongue.</td><td>Er denket, was er sprechen kann.</td></tr>
</table>

<table>
<tr><td colspan="2" align="center">**TAMINO, PAPAGENO**</td></tr>
<tr><td>And now they see we're both defiant</td><td>Sie müssen uns mit Scham verlassen,</td></tr>
<tr><td>They'll have to leave us, full of shame.</td><td>Es plaudert keiner sicherlich;</td></tr>
<tr><td>For Man is silent and he's strong . . .</td><td>Von festem Geiste ist ein Mann,</td></tr>
<tr><td>He knows the time to hold his tongue.</td><td>Er denket, was er sprechen kann.</td></tr>
</table>

<table>
<tr><td colspan="2" align="center">**PRIESTS**</td></tr>
<tr><td colspan="2" align="center">*(from within)*</td></tr>
<tr><td>The veil of our silence is broken!</td><td>Entweiht ist die heilige Schwelle!</td></tr>
<tr><td>Now banish the women who've spoken!</td><td>Hinab mit den Weibern zur Hölle!</td></tr>
</table>

A frightening chord resounds: all the instruments, rolls and claps of thunder and lightning; two claps of thunder at once.

<table>
<tr><td colspan="2" align="center">**THE THREE LADIES**</td></tr>
<tr><td>Away! Away! Away!</td><td>O weh! O weh! O weh!</td></tr>
</table>

They disappear through a trapdoor. Papageno falls to the ground in fear. He sings when the music is silent.

<table>
<tr><td colspan="2" align="center">**PAPAGENO**</td></tr>
<tr><td>Oh dear, oh dear, oh dear!</td><td>O weh! O weh! O weh!</td></tr>
</table>

The Threefold chord sounds. **Scene Six.** *Enter The Speaker and Second Priest with torches.*

THE SPEAKER

Tamino, we salute you. Your resolute behaviour has passed the first test. You have many more dangerous paths to follow but with the Gods' help you will succeed. [We go forward with a pure heart on our journey.] Follow me!

Heil dir, Jüngling! Dein standhaft männliches Betragen hat gesiegt. Zwar hast du noch manch rauhen und gefährlichen Weg zu wandern, den du aber durch Hilfe der Götter glücklich endigen wirst. Wir wollen also mit reinem Herzen unsere Wanderschaft weiter fortsetzen. So! Nun komm!

He places the sack over Tamino's head.

SECOND PRIEST

What's this, my friend? How are you feeling?

Was seh'ich! Freund, stehe auf! Wie ist dir?

PAPAGENO

Terrible.

Ich lieg' in einer Ohnmacht!

SECOND PRIEST

Stand up. Pull yourself together and be a man.

Auf! Sammle dich und sei ein Mann!

PAPAGENO
(standing up)

Oh well! I'll stand up, pull myself together, and be a man. [Why must I go through all this suffering and all these frights?] But if Papagena is already waiting for me, why do I have to go through so much to win her?

Aber sag't mir nur, meine Herren, warum muss ich denn alle diese Qualen und Schrecken empfinden? — Wenn mir ja die Götter eine Papagena bestimmten, warum denn mit so viel Gefahren sie erringen?

SECOND PRIEST

To prove that you deserve her. [*lit.* Your own intelligence should tell you the answer.] Come, it's my duty to lead you onwards.

Diese neugierige Frage mag deine Vernunft dir beantworten. Komm! Meine Pflicht heischt, dich weiter zu führen.

He places the sack over his head.

PAPAGENO

After so much exercise a man could lose his appetite for love altogether.

Bei so einer ewigen Wanderschaft möcht' einem wohl die Liebe auf immer vergehen!

Exeunt.

Transformation. *The scene changes to a delightful garden. Trees planted in a horseshoe pattern; in the centre stands a bower of flowers and roses, where Pamina is asleep. The moon shines on her face. In front of her is a smooth lawn.* **Scene Seven:** *enter Monostatos, who pauses, then sits down.*

MONOSTATOS

Ah, there she is, the prudish princess [And it is on account of this insignificant creature that they wanted to shred the soles of my feet! I have only the daylight to thank for having escaped with any skin left on them to tread on the ground. Hm! What was my offence anyway? That

Ha, da find'ich ja die spröde Schöne! Und um so einer geringen Pflanze wegen wollte man meine Fusssohlen behämmern? Also bloss dem heutigen Tag hab ich's zu verdanken, dass ich noch mit heiler Haut auf die Erde trete! Hm! Was war denn eigentlich mein

I fell in love with this exotic flower transplanted here from some foreign soil.] Who could not look at her and not be tempted, even if he came from a cooler climate than I do? This girl will drive me mad. The fire smouldering inside me will flare up and consume me. If I could be sure I was alone, I'd take the risk. [What a cursed foolish thing is love!] A surreptitious kiss couldn't do me any harm.

Verbrechen? Dass ich mich in eine Blume vergaffte, die auf fremdem Boden versetzt war? Und welcher Mensch, wenn er auch von gelinderem Himmelsstrich daherwanderte, würde bei so einem Anblick kalt und unempfindlich bleiben? Bei allen Sternen, das Mädchen wird mich noch um meinem Verstand bringen! Das Feuer, das in mir glimmt, wird mich noch verzehren. Wenn ich wüsste — dass ich so ganz allein und unbelauscht wäre, ich wagte es noch einmal. Es ist doch eine verdammte närrische Sache um die Liebe! Ein Küsschen, dächte ich, liesse sich entschuldigen.

Aria No. 13 [24]

All enjoy the beds of passion,
Cling, caress and stroke and kiss:
Why should I be out of fashion?
Only I'm denied the bliss.
I am black, that's why I'm hated.
I can love girls just as well.
Life for me without a woman
Is an ever-burning Hell.
I'll deny myself no longer
All the secret joys of love:
Fear is strong but lust is stronger,
Now the hawk desires the dove.
She lies there, and I am lusting —
Now I'll relish fierce desires.
If you find my love disgusting,
You can shut your stupid eyes.

Alles fühlt der Liebe Freuden,
Schnäbelt, tändelt, herzt und küsst;
Und ich sollt' die Liebe meiden,
Weil ein Schwarzer hässlich ist.
Ich bin auch den Mädchen gut!
Bin ich nicht von Fleisch und Blut?
Immer ohne Weibchen leben,
Wäre wahrlich Höllenglut!
Drum so will ich, weil ich lebe,
Schnäbeln, küssen, zärtlich sein!
Lieber guter Mond, vergebe,
Eine Weisse nahm mich ein
Weiss ist schön! Ich muss sie küssen;
Mond, verstecke dich dazu!
Sollt es dich zu sehr verdriessen,
O, so mach die Augen zu!

He creeps slowly and quietly towards Pamina.

Scene Eight. *The Queen of the Night appears, with a thunder clap, from the central trapdoor, so she stands just in front of Pamina.*

QUEEN

Away!   Zurück!

Pamina awakes. *

---

*Additional dialogue

PAMINA

Oh Gods!   Ihr Götter!

MONOSTATOS

(throwing himself into the shadows)

Oh woe! That is, if I am not mistaken, the goddess of the night.

O weh! Das ist — wo ich nicht irre, die Göttin der Nacht.

He stands still.

PAMINA

Mother! Mother! Mother!   Mutter! Mutter! Meine Mutter!

She falls into her arms.

MONOSTATOS

Mother? Hm! I must hear as much as I can of this.

Mutter? Hm! Dass muss man von weitem belauschen.

He hides.

QUEEN

Be thankful to the power which tore   Verdank es der Gewalt, mit der man dich

100

Where is the youth I sent you?	Wo ist der Jüngling, den ich nach dir sandte?

PAMINA

Oh, Mother he has left the world and gone to join Sarastro.	Ach, Mutter, der ist der Welt und den Menschen auf ewig entzogen. Er hat sich den Eingeweihten gewidmet.

QUEEN

[The initiates?] Miserable girl. Now you are lost to me for ever.	Den Eingeweihten? Unglückliche Tochter. Nun bist du auf ewig mir entrissen.

PAMINA

[Lost?] Dearest mother let us escape together; under your protection I'll brave any dangers.	Entrissen? O fliehen wir, liebe Mutter! Unter deinem Schutz trotz ich jeder Gefahr.

QUEEN

Protection! I cannot protect you any longer. I lost all my power when, on his deathbed your father gave the sevenfold circle of the sun to Sarastro and his followers. That all powerful circle Sarastro now wears on his breast.*	Schutz? Liebes Kind, deine Mutter kann dich nicht mehr schützen. Mit deines Vaters Tod ging meine Macht zu Grabe.

Footnote cont'd

you from me that you can still call me mother.	mir entriss, dass ich noch deine Mutter mich nenne.

* Original dialogue

PAMINA

My father . . .	Mein Vater . . .

QUEEN

Gave the sevenfold circle of the sun voluntarily to the Initiates. That powerful circle Sarastro now wears on his breast. When I tried to persuade him to change his mind, he replied with a wrinkled brow, 'Woman, my last hour is upon me — all my treasure is for you and your daughter'. 'The all piercing Circle of the Sun', said I, interrupting him hurriedly. 'That belongs to the Initiates', he answered. 'Sarastro will be the male guardian, just as I have been until now. And now no more; do not try to understand things which are inconceivable to a woman's mind. Your duty must be to commit yourself and your daughter to the authority of these men'.	Übergab freiwillig den siebenfachen Sonnenkreis den Eingeweihten. Diesen mächtigen Sonnenkreis trägt Sarastro auf seiner Brust. Als ich ihn darüber beredete, so sprach er mit gefalteter Stirn: Weib, meine letzte Stunde ist da — alle Schätze, so ich allein besass, sind dein und deiner Tochter. Der alles verzehrende Sonnen- kreis — fiel ich ihm hastig in die Rede — Ist den Geweihten bestimmt, antwortete er, Sarastro wird ihn so männlich verwalten wie ich bisher. Und nun kein Wort weiter; forsche nicht nach Wesen, die dem weiblichen Geist unbegreiflich sind. Deine Pflicht ist, dich und deine Tochter der Führung weiser Männer zu überlassen.

PAMINA

O dearly beloved mother! Must this young man also be lost to me forever?	Liebe Mutter, nach alledem zu schliessen, ist wohl auch der Jüngling auf immer für mich verloren?

QUEEN

Lost — unless you can persuade him to escape with you by the underground passages before the sun's rays warm the earth once again. The first light of day	Verloren, wenn du nicht, ehe die Sonne die Erde färbt, ihn durch diese unter- irdischen Gemächer zu fliehen beredest. Der erste Schimmer des Tages

PAMINA

But my father believed in these good
men and praised their goodness and their
wisdom. May I not continue to love
Tamino now that he has joined them?

QUEEN

You dare to defend those barbarians
and love a man who will join with
them to bring about my ruin?
Do you see this dagger? It was sharpened   Siehst du hier diesen Stahl? Er ist für
for Sarastro. Take it, kill him, and bring   Sarastro geschliffen, und du wirst ihn
back the circle of the sun to me.   töten und den mächtigen siebenfachen
       Sonnenkreis mir überliefern.

PAMINA

But mother . . .   Aber, liebste Mutter! —

QUEEN

Silence!   Kein Wort!

Aria No. 14 [25a, b]

I feel my heart aflame with hate and   Der Hölle Rache kocht in meinem
  murder.   Herzen,
Death and Destruction blaze around my   Tod und Verzweiflung flammet um mich
  throne.   her!
Should you not kill Sarastro as I order,   Fühlt nicht durch dich Sarastro
       Todesschmerzen,
You are no longer any child of mine,   So bist du meine Tochter nimmermehr —
And you shall be neither daughter nor
  my child.
I'll break our ties forever, renouncing   Verstossen sei auf ewig, verlassen sei auf
  you forever   ewig,
Abandoning forever any mother love or   Zertrümmert sei'n auf ewig alle Bande
  care.   der Natur,
If you won't kill Sarastro as I order,   Wenn nicht durch dich Sarastro wird
       erblassen!

Footnote cont'd

will decide you fate: either he is yours   entscheidet, ob er ganz dir oder den
alone, or he is handed over to be the   Eigeweihten gegeben ist.
prisoner of the Initiates.

PAMINA

Oh dearly beloved mother! Why can't I   Liebe Mutter, dürft' ich den Jüngling als
love this young man when he is an   Eingeweihten denn nicht auch ebenso
Initiate as tenderly as I do now? My   zärtlich lieben, wie ich ihn jetzt liebe?
father himself associated with these wise   Mein Vater selbst war ja mit diesen
men? He always spoke of them with joy   weisen Männern verbunden. Er sprach
extolling their excellence, their   jederzeit mit Entzücken von ihnen,
understanding, their virtue. Sarastro is   preiste ihre Güte — ihren Verstand —
no less virtuous.   ihre Tugend. Sarastro ist nicht weniger
       tugendhaft.

QUEEN

What do I hear? You, my own daughter,   Was hör ich! Du, meine Tochter,
are able to defend the ignominious   könntest die schändlichen Gründe dieser
principles of these barbarians? Would   Barbaren verteidigen? So einen Mann
you love a man in alliance with my   lieben, der, mit meinem Todfeind
mortal enemy who would at any   verbunden, mit jedem Augenblick nur
moment send me to my death?   meinen Sturz bereiten würde?

102

Hear, God of Vengeance! Hear a mother's vow.	Hört! Rachegötter! Hört der Mutter Schwur!

She disappears.* Monostatos returns.

PAMINA

She swore to forsake me but how could I
kill Sarastro? . . . Monostatos!

MONOSTATOS

I have heard everything. Now both you
and your mother are in my power. But if
you swear to love me I will be indulgent.

PAMINA

Monostatos, I implore you!

MONOSTATOS

Choose love or death. Your life is at
stake!

---

*Original Sequence

Scene Nine.

PAMINA
(the dagger in her hand)

Commit murder! Oh gods! I cannot. I cannot.	Morden soll ich? Götter! Das kann ich nicht — das kann ich nicht.

She stands in thought. **Scene Ten.** *Monostatos approaches fast, furtively and very gleefully.*

MONOSTATOS

So Sarastro's Circle of the Sun has its uses? And to obtain it, the lovely girl must kill him. That serves my purpose.	Sarastros Sonnenkreis hat also auch seine Wirkung? Und diesen zu erhalten, soll das schöne Mädchen ihn mordern. Das ist Salz in meine Suppe.

PAMINA

Didn't my mother swear by all the gods that she would forsake me if I did not use this dagger against Sarastro? O Gods! What should I do?	Aber schwur sie nicht bei allen Göttern, mich zu verstossen, wenn ich den Dolch nicht gegen Sarastro kehre? Götter! Was soll ich tun?

MONOSTATOS

Trust in me!	Dich mir anvertraun.

He takes the dagger from her. Pamina screams.

Why do you tremble? Because I am black or because of your criminal intent?	Warum zitterst du? Vor meiner schwarzen Farbe oder vor dem ausgedachten Mord?

PAMINA
(timidly)

So you know!	Du weiss also?

MONOSTATOS

Everything! I know that your fate, and that of your mother also are in my hands. I have only to say a single word to Sarastro and your mother would be plunged in those vaults of water where the Initiates are, so they say, purified. She would never emerge unharmed from these caverns, unless I so decided. So there is only one way open to you to save yourself and your mother.	Alles. Ich weiss sogar, dass nicht nur dein, sondern auch deiner Mutter Leben in meiner Hand steht. Ein einziges Wort sprech ich zu Sarastro, und deine Mutter wird in diesem Gewölb', in dem Wasser, das die Eingeweihten reinigen soll, wie man sagt, ersäuft. Aus diesem Gewölb' kommt sie nun sicher nicht mehr mit heiler Haut, wenn ich es will. Du hast also nur einen Weg, dich und deine Mutter zu retten.

Enter Sarastro

MONOSTATOS

Sir, I am innocent.

Footnote cont'd

PAMINA

And that is?	Der wäre?

MONOSTATOS

To love me!	Mich zu lieben!

PAMINA
(trembling, to herself)

Oh Gods!	Götter!

MONOSTATOS
(happily)

The storm bends the little sapling towards me. Well, maiden, yes or no!	Das junge Bäumchen jagt der Sturm auf meine Seite. Nun, Mädchen, ja oder nein!

PAMINA
(passionately)

No!	Nein!

MONOSTATOS
(angrily)

No? And the reason? Because I am the colour of a black phantom? No! Ha! You will die!	Nein? Und warum? Weil ich die Farbe eines schwarzen Gespenstes trage? Nicht? Ha! So stirb!

He seizes her by the hand.

PAMINA

Monostatos, see me here on my knees — spare me!	Monostatos, sieh mich hier auf meinen Knien — schone meiner!

MONOSTATOS

Love or death! Speak! Your life is at the point of this blade!	Liebe oder Tod! Sprich! Dein Leben steht auf der Spitze.

PAMINA

I have offered my heart to the Prince.	Mein Herz hab ich dem Jüngling geopfert.

MONOSTATOS

What do I care for your 'offer'? — Speak!	Was kümmert mich dein Opfer — sprich!

PAMINA

Never!	Nie!

Scene Eleven: *Sarastro enters.*

MONOSTATOS

So, die!	So fahre denn hin!

Sarastro pushes him away roughly.

Sir, do not punish me. This is not my plot, I am innocent. They swore to kill you, and I wanted to avenge you.	Herr, mein Unternehmen ist nicht strafbar, ich bin unschuldig! Man hat deinen Tod geschworen, darum wollte ich dich rächen.

SARASTRO

I know this only too well. I know your soul is as black as your face. And I would punish you with the greatest severity for this black conspiracy, if I did not know that it was a woman, as evil as her daughter is virtuous, who forged the dagger for the murder. Thanks to the wickedness of this woman's machinations, I will let you go free. Go!	Ich weiss nur allzuviel, weiss, dass deine Seele ebenso schwarz als dein Gesicht ist. Auch würde ich dies schwarze Unternehmen mit höchster Strenge an dir bestrafen, wenn nicht ein böses Weib, das zwar eine sehr gute Tochter hat, den Dolch dazu geschmiedet hätte. Verdank es der bösen Handlung des Weibes, dass du ungestraft davonziehst. Geh!

SARASTRO

Your soul is as black as your face. Go!

MONOSTATOS

If I can't have the daughter, I'll try my luck with the mother!	Jetzt such'ich die Mutter auf, weil die Tochter mir nicht beschieden ist.

Exit Monostatos. **Scene Twelve**

PAMINA

Sir, do not punish my mother. Her grief at my absence has sent her mad.	Herr, strafe meine Mutter nicht! Der Schmerz über meine Abwesenheit —

SARASTRO

I know everything. She is planning vengeance on me and all humanity. By her own laws she deserves to be punished. But we follow different rules.	Ich weiss Alles.*

Aria No. 15 [26]

To rule by Hate and Vengeance	In diesen heil'gen Hallen
Is not our practice here,	Kennt man die Rache nicht,
And if a man's repentant	Und ist ein Mensch gefallen,
He's saved by love, not fear.	Führt Liebe ihn zur Pflicht.
If he is lost a loving hand	Dann wandelt er an Freundes Hand
Shows him with joy our happy land.	Vergnügt und froh ins bess're Land.
Here Peace and Mercy govern,	In diesen heil'gen Mauern,
By Love alone we live,	Wo Mensch den Menschen liebt,
Though tyrants rage and threaten	Kann kein Verräter lauern,
We love them and forgive.	Weil man dem Feind vergibt.
If man can't learn what love can do	Wen solche Lehren nicht erfreun,
His days on earth are surely few.	Verdienet nicht, ein Mensch zu sein.

Exeunt.

Transformation. *The scene changes to a great hall, in which the flying machine can turn. The flying machine has a door and is decorated with roses and flowers. In the foreground are two grassy platforms.* **Scene Thirteen.** *Tamino and Papageno with their heads uncovered are led in by the two priests.*

THE SPEAKER

We shall leave you both alone here. When the trumpets sound, you must continue in that direction. Farewell Prince, and remember your vow of silence.	Hier seid ihr euch beide allein überlassen. — Sobald die Posaune tönt, dann nehm't ihr euren Weg dahin! — Prinz, leb't wohl! Wir sehen uns, eh' ihr ganz am Ziele seid, Noch einmal vergesst das Wort nicht: Schweigen!

---

*

I know everything. I know that she is wandering in the vaults beneath the temple, conceiving plans of revenge on me and all humanity. You alone will see how I am avenged on your mother. May Heaven give the pleasing young man courage and constancy in his purpose, so that you may share his good fortune. Then your mother will have to retire in disgrace to her palace.	Ich weiss alles. Weiss, dass sie in unterirdischen Gemächern des Tempels herumirrt und Rache über mich und die Menschheit kocht. Allein du sollst sehen, wie ich mich an deiner Mutter räche. Der Himmel schenke nur dem holden Jüngling Mut und Standhaftigkeit in seinem Vorsatz, dann bist du mit ihm glücklich, und deine Mutter soll beschämt nach ihrer Burg zurückkehren.

Exit.

SECOND PRIEST

Papageno, remember, whoever breaks silence in this place will be struck down by thunder and lightning. Farewell.

Papageno! Wer an diesem Ort sein Stillschweigen bricht, den strafen die Götter durch Donner und Blitz. Leb' wohl!

Exit. Scene Fourteen. Tamino sits on a grassy bank.

PAPAGENO
(after a pause)

Tamino!

Tamino!

TAMINO

Sh!

St!

PAPAGENO

Oh, this is a fine sort of life. Back [in my straw-hut or] in the woods I could at least hear the birds chirrup.

Das ist ein lustiges Leben! — Wär'ich lieber in meiner Strohhütte, oder im Wald, so hört'ich doch manchmal einen Vogel pfeifen!

TAMINO

Sh!

St!

PAPAGENO

Surely I can talk to myself if I want to? [and we two can talk together — we're men.]

Mit mir selbst werd' ich wohl sprechen dürfen; und auch wir zwei können zusammen sprechen — wir sind ja Männer.

TAMINO

Sh!

St!

PAPAGENO
(singing)

LA LA LA . . . They don't even offer you a drop of water in this place, let alone anything stronger!

La la la — la la la! — Nicht einmal einen Tropfen Wasser bekommt man bei diesen Leuten, viel weniger sonst was.

Scene Fifteen. An ugly old woman enters with a large goblet of water.

PAPAGENO
(looking at her for a long time)

Hallo! Oh Hallo!
Is that for me?

Ist das für mich?

OLD WOMAN

Yes, my angel!

Ja, mein Engel!

PAPAGENO
(looks at her again and drinks)

Thank you.

OLD WOMAN

No trouble at all.

PAPAGENO

Ugh . . . water!

Nicht mehr und nicht weniger als Wasser.

106

OLD WOMAN	
Thank you kindly.	

PAPAGENO	
No trouble at all. Tell me, mysterious beauty, do you entertain all strangers like this?	Sag' du mir, du unbekannte Schöne, werden alle fremden Gäste auf diese Art bewirtet?

OLD WOMAN	
Certainly, my angel.	Freilich, mein Engel!

PAPAGENO	
In that case, I don't suppose you see many visitors?	So, so! — Auf diese Art werden die Fremden auch nicht gar zu häufig kommen.

OLD WOMAN	
Very few!	Sehr wenig.

PAPAGENO	
I can believe that. Come on, old lady, come and talk to me. I'm bored out of my feathers. Tell me, how old are you?	Kann mir's denken. — Geh', Alte, setze dich her zu mir! mir ist die Zeit verdammt lange. Sag' du mir, wie alt bist du denn?

OLD WOMAN	
How old am I?	Wie alt?

PAPAGENO	
Yes!	Ja!

OLD WOMAN	
Eighteen years and two minutes.	Achtzehn Jahr' und zwei Minuten.

PAPAGENO	
[Eighty years and two minutes?]*	

OLD WOMAN	
[EIGHTEEN years and two minutes!]	

PAPAGENO	
Ha ha ha! Is that so my little angel? Have you got a boy-friend?	Ha ha ha! — Ei, du junger Engel! Hast du auch einen Geliebten?

OLD WOMAN	
Oh, certainly!	I, freilich!

PAPAGENO	
Is he as young as you are?	Ist er auch so jung wie du?

OLD WOMAN	
Not quite. He is ten years older.	Nicht gar; er ist um zehn Jahre älter.

PAPAGENO	
Ten years older? That must be a fiery passion.	Um zehn Jahre, ist er älter als du? Das muss eine Liebe sein!

OLD WOMAN	
Oh yes.	

* A joke traditional in many German productions.

PAPAGENO	
What's your boy-friend called?	Wie nennt sich denn dein Liebhaber?

OLD WOMAN	
Papageno!	Papageno!

PAPAGENO
(screams, then a pause)

Papageno? PAPAGENO? Where is he, this Papageno?	Papageno? — Wo ist er denn, dieser Papageno?

OLD WOMAN	
Standing right here, my angel.	Da steht er, mein Engel.

PAPAGENO	
You mean that I'm your boy-friend?	Ich wär' dein Geliebter?

OLD WOMAN	
Of course, my angel!	Ja, mein Engel!

PAPAGENO
(quickly taking the water and splashing her face with it)

Then, tell me, what's your name?	Sag' du mir, wie heisst du denn?

OLD WOMAN	
My name is . . .	Ich heisse —

A violent thunder clap. The old woman limps hurriedly away. Tamino stands up and reproaches him with his finger.

PAPAGENO	
Oh Gods, forgive me! I won't say another word as long as I live!	O weh! Nun sprech ich kein Wort mehr!

Scene Sixteen. *The Three Boys enter in a flying machine, decorated with roses. In the centre is a beautifully laid table. One of the boys carries the flute; another the music box with the bells. | Trio No. 16*

THE THREE BOYS [27]

Twice now we've gladly come to meet you	Seid uns zum zweitenmal willkommen,
Seeking you where Sarastro dwells.	Ihr Männer, in Sarastros Reich.
He bade us find you and, in greeting,	Er schickt, was man euch abgenommen,
Sends you the flute and magic bells.	Die Flöte und die Glöckchen euch.
Now you have suffered thirst and fasting	Wollt ihr die Speisen nicht verschmähen,
He bids you eat and drink your fill.	So esset, trinket froh davon.
We shall return a third and last time,	Wenn wir zum drittenmal uns sehen,
Joy shall reward your steadfast will.	Ist Freude eures Mutes Lohn!
You must be brave and fear no ill.	Tamino, Mut! Nah ist das Ziel.
You Papageno, silence still.	Du Papageno, schweige still!

While the Boys are singing, they put the table on the stage. The Boys fly off. **Scene Seventeen.**

PAPAGENO	
Tamino, aren't you [we] going to eat anything?	Tamino, wollen wir nicht speisen?

Tamino plays the flute

Oh, you whistle on your flute and I'll wet my whistle. Ah, this wine is fit for the Gods. Let's see whether Mr.	Blase du nur fort auf deiner Flöte; ich will meine Brocken blasen! Herr Sarastro führt eine gute Küche. Auf diese Art,

Sarastro's kitchen is as good as his cellar. Mm. The food's wonderful too — even I don't mind keeping quiet when my mouth is full.

ja, da will ich schon schweigen, wenn ich immer solche gute Bissen bekomme — Nun, ich will sehen, ob auch der Keller so gut bestellt ist. Ha! das ist Götterwein!

Scene Eighteen. *Enter Pamino. Tamino stops playing the flute.*

PAMINA
(joyfully)

You're here Tamino. I heard the sound of your flute and hurried to find you. But you look sad. Won't you speak to me?

Du hier? — Gütige Götter! Dank euch, dass ihr mich diesen Weg führtet. Ich hörte deine Flöte — und so lief ich pfeilschnell dem Tone nach — Aber du bist traurig? Sprichst nicht eine Silbe mit deiner Pamina?

Tamino sighs.

[What's this? Must you shun me?] Won't you tell me you still love me?

Wie? Ich soll dich meiden? Liebst du mich nicht mehr?

Tamino sighs and waves her away.

Do you want me to go away without knowing why? Tamino, what have I done? Don't make me suffer. [I look for trust and help from you — and would you make my loving heart suffer still more?]

Ich soll fliehen, ohne zu wissen warum? Tamino! Holder Jüngling! Hab ich dich beleidigt? O kränke mein Herz nicht noch mehr. Bei dir such ich Trost, Hilfe — und du kannst mein liebevolles Herz noch mehr kränken? Liebst du mich nicht mehr?

(Tamino sighs.)

Papageno can you tell me what has happened to Tamino? You too? At least explain your silence to me.

Papageno, sag du mir, was ist mit meinem Freund? Wie? Auch du? Erkläre mir wenigstens die Ursache eures Stillschweigens?

Papageno waves her away with both hands, his mouth full of food.

Oh, this is worse than suffering, worse than death. [Beloved, my only Tamino.]

O, das ist mehr als Kränkung, mehr als Tod! Liebster, einziger Tamino!

Aria No. 17

PAMINA [28]

Ah, I know that all is ended.
Gone forever the joy of love.
Never will those hours of beauty
Come again to fill my heart.
See Tamino, see my weeping tears
That flow for you alone.
Just one word to say you love me,
Or I'll find rest in Death alone.

Ach, ich fühl's, es ist verschwunden,
Ewig hin mein ganzes Glück!
Nimmer kommt ihr, Wonnestunden,
Meinem Herzen mehr zurück!
Sieh, Tamino, diese Tränen
Fliessen, Trauter, dir allein.
Fühlst du nicht der Liebe Sehnen,
So wird Ruh im Tode sein!

Exit Pamina. **Scene Nineteen**

PAPAGENO
(eating greedily)

There, you see, Tamino, I can keep quiet too when it suits me! Yes, when it comes to important things, I'm a man!

Nicht wahr, Tamino, ich kann auch schweigen, wenn's sein muss? — Ja, bei so einem Unternehmen bin ich Mann.

(He drinks.)

I drink to the health of the head cook and the butler!

Der Herr Koch und der Herr Keller meister sollen leben!

First Threefold Chord. Tamino indicates to Papageno to come along.

You go ahead, I'll follow when I've finished. [It takes more courage to stay!]

Geh' du nur voraus, ich komme schon nach! Der Stärkere bleibt da!

Tamino warns him and goes out by the opposite side of the stage from which he entered.

Now I can enjoy my supper in peace. Why should I rush off just when my taste buds are tingling? Wild animals couldn't drag me away from this. [I won't even go if Mr. Sarastro sets his six lions on me.]

Jetzt will ich mir's erst recht wohl sein lassen. Da ich in meinem besten Appetit bin, soll ich gehen? Das lass ich wohl bleiben. Ich ging' jetzt nicht fort, und wenn Herr Sarastro seine sechs Löwen an mich spannte.

The lions appear; Papageno is frightened.

[Oh gods, have pity on me!]
Oh, Tamino, save me, help! help!
[These Mister lions intend to make a mouthful of me.]

O Barmherzigkeit, ihr gütigen Götter!
Tamino, rette mich! Die Herren Löwen machen eine Mahlzeit aus mir.

Tamino returns hurriedly and plays his flute. The lions go away; he makes a sign to Papageno.

You and that flute have saved my life. I promise I'll come with you in future.*

Second Threefold Chord

There they go again! All right, we're coming! Don't be in such a hurry . . . I'll just go and have another nibble.

Animals growl

Oh go away and find a mouse to frighten.

Animals growl again. Third Threefold Chord.

Oh. . . !

Papageno screams, exit with table.

Transformation. *The scene changes into the vault of a pyramid. The Speaker and other priests. Two priests carry an illuminated pyramid on their shoulders; other priests hold transparent lamps in the shape of pyramids in their hands.* **Scene Twenty.** *Eighteen priests stand in a triangle, six to each side | Chorus No. 18*

CHORUS [29]

Oh, Isis and Osiris, Gods resplendent!
The darkness fades; the blazing sun's transcendent.
Soon now this brave young man will find a new life;
Soon too within these walls he'll find a true love.

O, Isis und Osiris, welche Wonne!
Die düstre Nacht verscheucht der Glanz der Sonne.
Bald fühlt der edle Jüngling neues Leben;
Bald ist er unserem Dienste ganz ergeben.

---

* Original Text.

I'm coming. Call me a rascal it I don't follow you everywhere.

Ich gehe schon! Heiss du mich einen Schelm, wenn ich dir nicht in allem folge.

Second Threefold Chord.

There we go again. We're coming soon. But tell me, Tamino, what will become of us?

Das geht uns an. Wir kommen schon. Aber hör einmal, Tamino was wird denn noch alles mit uns werden?

Tamino points to the heavens.

Must I ask the Gods?

Die Götter soll ich fragen?

Tamino nods.

Ah, yes! The Gods can obviously tell us more than we know!

Ja, die könnten uns freilich mehr sagen als wir wissen.

Third Threefold Chord. Tamino drags Papageno away.

What's the hurry? We will only arrive in good time to be broiled.

Eile nur nicht so, wir kommen noch immer zeitig genug, um uns braten zu lassen.

Exeunt.

| His heart is chaste, his soul is pure. | Sein Geist is kühn, sein Herz ist rein, |
| Soon he will join us, cleansed and pure. | Bald wird er unser würdig sein. |

Scene twenty-one. *Tamino is brought before the assembly.*

SARASTRO

Tamino, so far you have borne yourself	Prinz, dein Betragen war bis hierher
with manly composure, but you still have	männlich und gelassen; nun hast du noch
two more dangerous paths to follow. If	zwei gefährliche Wege zu wandern.
you still love Pamina and wish to rule	Schlägt dein Herz noch ebenso warm
as a wise and enlightened sovereign, the	für Pamina und wünschest du einst als
gods will go with you. [Your hand!]	ein weiser Fürst zu regieren, so mögen
Bring in Pamina.	die Götter dich ferner begleiten. Deine
	Hand! Man bringe Pamina!

Silence falls upon the priests. Pamina is brought in. She wears the sack reserved for the Initiates. Sarastro loosens the thongs which hold on the sack.

PAMINA

| [Where am I? What a dreadful silence! | Wo bin ich? Welch eine fürchterliche |
| Sarastro,] Tell me, where is Tamino? | Stille! Sarastro, wo ist mein Jüngling? |

SARASTRO

| He is waiting to take a last farewell. | Er wartet deiner, um dir das letzte |
| | Lebewohl zu sagen. |

PAMINA

| A last farewell. Oh, where is he? Let me | Das letzte Lebewohl? Oh, wo ist er? |
| see him. | Führt mich zu ihm. |

SARASTRO

| He is here. | Hier. |

PAMINA

| Tamino. | Tamino! |

TAMINO

| Pamina, stay there. | Zurück! |

Trio No. 19 [30]

PAMINA

| My only joy, ah, must we part? | Soll ich dich, Teurer, nicht mehr sehn? |

SARASTRO

| You need not fear, but trust his heart. | Ihr werdet froh euch wiedersehn! |

PAMINA

| I fear the dangers that may harm you. | Dein warten tödliche Gefahren! |

TAMINO

| I trust the truth to guard and arm me. | Die Götter mögen mich bewahren! |

PAMINA

| I fear the dangers that may harm you. | Dein warten tödliche Gefahren! |

TAMINO, SARASTRO

$\left.\begin{matrix} I \\ Now \end{matrix}\right\}$ trust the truth to guard and arm $\left\{\begin{matrix} me. \\ him. \end{matrix}\right.$ Die Götter mögen $\left\{\begin{matrix} ihn \\ mich \end{matrix}\right\}$ bewahren!

111

PAMINA

I hear a dreadful voice of warning	Du wirst dem Tode nicht entgehen,
That makes me long for you to stay.	Mir flüstert dieses Ahnung ein.

TAMINO, SARASTRO

I serve the lovely Gods of Morning —	Der Götter Wille mag geschehen,
Where they command, {I / he} must obey.	Ihr Wink soll {mir / ihm} Gesetze sein!

PAMINA

Oh, if you knew true love's devotion,	O liebtest du, wie ich dich liebe,
You could not stay so firm and calm.	Du würdest nicht so ruhig sein.

TAMINO, SARASTRO

Trust me, {I feel / he feels} the same emotion,	Glaub mir, {ich fühle / er fühlet} gleiche Triebe,
And know that love need fear no harm.	Wird ewig dein Getreuer sein!

SARASTRO

The hour has struck, his trials are starting.	Die Stunde schlägt, nun müsst ihr scheiden!

PAMINA, TAMINO

How grievous are the pangs of parting.	Wie bitter sind der Trennung Leiden!

SARASTRO

Tamino now must take his leave.	Tamino muss nun wieder fort.

TAMINO

Pamina, I must really leave.	Pamina, ich muss wirklich fort!

PAMINA

Tamino, must you really leave?	Tamino muss nun wirklich fort?

SARASTRO

Now he must leave.	Nun muss er fort!

TAMINO

Now I must leave.	Nun muss ich fort.

PAMINA

So you must leave?	So musst du fort!

TAMINO

Pamina, fare you well.	Pamina, lebe wohl!

PAMINA

Tamino, fare you well.	Tamino, lebe wohl!

SARASTRO

So leave her now	Nun eile fort.
And keep your vow:	Dich ruft dein Wort.
The hour is come, for you must leave now.	Die Stunde schlägt, wir sehn uns wieder!

PAMINA, TAMINO

Ah, peace of spirit, gone forever!	Ach, goldne Ruhe, kehre wieder!
Fare you well, fare you well!	Lebe wohl! Lebe wohl!

SARASTRO

But not forever!	Wir sehn uns wieder.

They separate. **Scene Twenty-two.**

PAPAGENO
(off stage)

Tamino, Tamino! Don't desert me!	Tamino! Tamino! Willst du mich denn gänzlich verlassen?

(He enters searching for Tamino)

I promise I won't leave you again! [If only I knew where I was! As long as I live I won't leave you again!] Don't leave me alone in the dark.	Wenn ich nur wenigstens wüsste, wo ich wäre! Tamino! Tamino! So lang' ich lebe, bleib' ich nicht mehr von dir! Nur diesmal verlass' mich armen Reisege-fährten nicht!

He goes up to the door through which Tamino has just passed.

A VOICE

Go back!	Zurück!

Then, with a clap of thunder, a flame bursts from the door, and there is a loud chord.

PAPAGENO

[Merciful Gods! Where can I turn?] All right, I'm going. If only I knew where I came from. Tamino!	Barmherzige Götter! Wo wend' ich mich hin? Wenn ich nur wüsste, wo ich hereinkam!

He retreats to the door through which he entered.

THE VOICE

Go back!	Zurück!

A thunderclap, flames and chord as before.

PAPAGENO
(crying)

Now they won't let me go forwards or backwards. I suppose they want me to die of starvation. I knew I was wrong to come on this trip.	Nun kann ich weder vorwärts noch zurück! Muss vielleicht am Ende gar verhungern! Schon recht! Warum bin ich mitgereist!

Scene Twenty-three. *Enter the Speaker carrying his pyramid.*

THE SPEAKER

Papageno, you deserve to go wandering in the bowels of the earth for ever. But the gods have taken pity on you though you will now never know true enlightenment.	Mensch! Du hättest verdient, auf immer in finstern Klüften der Erde zu wandern — die gütigen Götter aber entlassen dich der Strafe. Dafür aber wirst du has himmlische Vergnügen der Eingeweihten nie fühlen.

PAPAGENO

Well I shan't be alone in that. There are lots of other folk like me. We prefer wine to wisdom.	Je nun, es gibt noch mehr Leute meinesgleichen! Mir wäre jetzt ein gut Glas Wein das grösste Vergnügen.

THE SPEAKER

Is that all you want from life?	Sonst hast du keinen Wunsch in dieser Welt?

PAPAGENO

Just at the moment, yes. I'll settle for a nice cool drink.	Bis jetzt nicht.

THE SPEAKER

There you are then.	Man wird dich damit bedienen!

Exit the Speaker. A large goblet of red wine appears from the ground.

PAPAGENO

That's what I call service. Marvellous! Divine! [Heavenly!] I feel so cheerful I could soar right up to the sun if only I had wings. I'm beginning to feel so happy. But there's something missing . . . something I need. I wonder what it is . . . Ah yes!

Juchhe! da ist er schon! Herrlich! Himmlisch! Göttlich! Ha! ich bin jetzt so vergnügt, dass ich bis zur Sonne fliegen wollte, wenn ich Flügel hätte! Ha! Mir wird ganz wunderlich um's Herz! Ich möchte — ich wünschte — ja, was denn?

Aria No. 20 [31]

PAPAGENO

(while singing, he plays his magic bells)

I'd like a wife to hug me
And keep me warm at night —
A girl who'd really love me
Is Papageno's right, that's Papageno's right.
Then living would give me such pleasure
That Princes would envy my treasure,

I'd know the true meaning of life
If Heaven would find me a wife.
Oh, please find me a wife.

Ein Mädchen oder Weibchen
Wünscht Papageno sich!
O, so ein sanftes Täubchen
Wär' Seligkeit für mich!

Dann schmekte mir Trinken und Essen,
[32]
Dann könnt ich mit Fürsten mich messen,
Des Lebens als Weiser mich freun,
Und wie im Elysium sein.

I'd like a wife to hug me
And keep me warm at night —
A girl who'd really love me
Is Papageno's right, that's Papageno's right.
Oh, am I then really so ugly
That no pretty girl wants to love me?
Unless a young girl shares my bed
I'd really be better off dead.

Ein Mädchen oder Weibchen
Wünscht Papageno sich!
O, so ein sanftes Täubchen
Wär' Seligkeit für mich!
Ach, kann ich denn keiner von allen
Den reizenden Mädchen gefallen?
Helf' eine mir nur aus der Not,
Sonst gräm ich mich wahrlich zu Tod.

I'd like a wife to hug me
And keep me warm at night —
A girl who'd really love me
Is Papageno's right, that's Papageno's right.
If all you young ladies still spurn me,
The fire of my passion will burn me.
But if one will give me a kiss,
My heartache will turn into bliss.

Ein Mädchen oder Weibchen
Wünscht Papageno sich!
O, so ein sanftes Täubchen
Wär' Seligkeit für mich!
Wird keine mir Liebe gewähren,
So muss mich die Flamme verzehren!
Doch küsst mich ein weiblicher Mund,
So bin ich schon wieder gesund!

Scene Twenty-four. *The Old Woman enters dancing and leaning on her stick.*

OLD WOMAN

Here I am, my angel.

Da bin ich schon, mein Engel!

PAPAGENO

So you've decided to take pity on me? That's just my luck!

Du hast dich meiner erbarmt? Das ist mein Glück!

OLD WOMAN

Yes, my angel, and if you promise to be faithful to me, you'll see what a tender little wife I will be.

Ja, mein Engel! Und wenn du mir versprichst, mir ewig treu zu bleiben, dann sollst du sehen, wie zärtlich dein Weibchen dich lieben wird.

PAPAGENO

Oh, you sweet little thing, you.	Ei, du zärtliches Närrchen!

OLD WOMAN

I'll fondle you and embrace you [and kiss your lips] and press you to my lips [heart].	O, wie will ich dich umarmen, dich liebkosen, dich an mein Herz drücken?

PAPAGENO

[Only to your heart?]	Auch an's Herz drücken.

OLD WOMAN

Now give me your hand to seal our bargain.	Komm', reich mir zum Pfand unseres Bundes deine Hand!

PAPAGENO

Not so fast, my dearest. A decision like that needs some thought.	Nur nicht so hastig, lieber Engel! So ein Bündnis braucht doch auch seine Überlegung.

OLD WOMAN

Papageno, I advise you not to hesitate. Give me your hand or you'll be locked up here for ever.	Papageno, ich rate dir, zaud're nicht! Deine Hand, oder du bist auf immer hier eingekerkert.

PAPAGENO

Locked up!	Eingekerkert?

OLD WOMAN

Bread and water will be your only food. You'll never see either man *or* woman and you'll have to abandon the world for ever.	Wasser und Brot wird deine tägliche Kost sein. Ohne Freund, ohne Freundin musst du leben und der Welt auf immer entsagen.

PAPAGENO

Only water to drink? Abandon the world? Oh well, better an old girl than no girl at all. Well, there's my hand then, and I promise to be faithful to you . . .	Wasser trinken? Der Welt entsagen? Nein, da will ich doch lieber eine Alte nehmen, als gar keine. Nun, da hast du meine Hand mit der Versicherung, dass ich dir immer getreu bleibe,

(aside)

as long as I don't find anyone prettier.	so lang' ich keine Schönere sehe.

OLD WOMAN

You promise?	Das schwörst du?

PAPAGENO

I promise . . .	Ja, das schwör' ich!

The Old Woman turns into Papagena, dressed like Papageno.

Pa-Pa-Papagena!	Pa-Pa-Papagena!

Papageno goes to embrace her. **Scene Twenty-five.** *The Speaker holds her firmly back.*

THE SPEAKER

Away with you, young woman. He still is not yet worthy of you!	Fort mit dir, junges Weib! Er ist deiner noch nicht würdig! Zurück! sag' ich, oder zittre!

The Speaker takes her away; Papageno wants to follow them.

115

PAPAGENO

Oooh! Will you kindly stop interfering in
my family affairs. That's a bird I'm
going to catch . . . even if the earth
swallows me up! [Oh Gods!]

Eh' ich mich zurückziehe, soll die Erde
mich verschlingen. O ihr Götter!

Papageno disappears in a hole which has opened at his feet.

Transformation. *The scene changes to a little garden.* **Scene Twenty-six.** / *Finale No. 21*

THE THREE BOYS [33]

The sun arises like a vision
And brings a brighter morn;
It ends the reign of superstition —
The day of Truth will dawn.
Let no dark evil now affright men.
Let Truth now shine here and delight
    them.
Then every man shall scorn to lie,
Then Truth shall live and Death shall die.

Bald prangt, den Morgen zu verkünden,
Die Sonn' auf goldner Bahn!
Bald soll der Aberglaube schwinden,
Bald siegt der weise Mann.
O holde Ruhe, steig hernieder,
Kehr in der Menschen Herzen wieder;

Dann wird die Erd' ein Himmelreich,
Und Sterbliche den Göttern gleich.

FIRST BOY

But see, some sorrow grieves Pamina!

Doch seht, Verzweiflung quält Paminen.

SECOND, THIRD BOYS

What troubles her?

Wo ist sie denn?

FIRST BOY

She seems tormented.

Sie ist von Sinnen.

THE THREE BOYS

It's love that makes her feel this torture.
Let's try to help and reassure her.
Pamina's pain is our pain too —
Though we but guess what Love can do.
She comes; let's wait in hiding here
Until her purpose is more clear.

Sie quält verschmähter Liebe Leiden.
Lasst uns der Armen Trost bereiten!
Fürwahr, ihr Schicksal geht uns nah!
O wäre nur ihr Jüngling da! —
Sie kommt, lasst uns beseite gehn,
Damit wir, was sie mache, sehn.

Scene Twenty-seven. *Pamina enters, as if she has lost her wits, with a dagger in her hand.*
They hide. [34]

PAMINA

And so a knife must wed me now?
Embracing you, I keep my vow.

Du also bist mein Bräutigam?
Durch dich vollend' ich meinen Gram!

THE THREE BOYS
(aside)

What were those fearful words she said?
I fear her love has made her mad.

Welch dunkle Worte sprach sie da?
Die Arme ist dem Wahnsinn nah.

PAMINA

Ah see, my love, I'll be your bride,
Our wedding knot will soon be tied.

Geduld mein Trauter, ich bin dein,
Bald werden wir vermählet sein.

THE THREE BOYS

Madness leads her to destruction —
Suicide's her sure intention!

Wahnsinn tobt ihr im Gehirne;
Selbstmord steht auf ihrer Stirne. —
(to Pamina)

Sweet young lady — See us here!

Holdes Mädchen, sieh uns an!

PAMINA

I will die now, since Tamino,	Sterben will ich, weil der Mann,
Who said he'd always love me,	Den ich nimmermehr kann hassen,
Means to break the vow he gave me.	Seine Traute kann verlassen.

(showing the dagger)

See, my mother gave this knife!	Dies gab meine Mutter mir.

THE THREE BOYS

Don't forget. God gave you life!	Selbstmord strafet Gott an dir.

PAMINA

Better far to end this anguish	Lieber durch dies Eisen sterben,
Than to live alone and languish.	Als durch Liebesgram verderben.
Mother, Mother! Your curse makes me wild,	Mutter, durch dich leide ich,
And your knife destroys your child.	Und dein Fluch verfolget mich.

THE THREE BOYS

Wait though! Wait and come with us!	Mädchen, willst du mit uns gehn?

PAMINA

Ah! my cup of grief is full —	Ha, des Jammers Mass ist voll!
False Tamino fare you well.	Falscher Jüngling, lebe wohl!
See Pamina will not lie:	Sieh, Pamina stirbt durch dich:
Love's forsworn, I swear I'll die!	Dieses Eisen töte mich.

She raises the dagger to stab herself.

THE THREE BOYS
(preventing her)

Wait, unhappy girl, oh wait!	Ha, Unglückliche! Halt ein!
If you kill yourself through sorrow	Sollte dies dein Jüngling sehen,
Then your love will die tomorrow,	Würde er vor Gram vergehn;
For his grief will be so great!	Denn er liebt dich allein.

PAMINA
(recovering herself)

What! You say that he adores me,	Was? Er fühlte Gegenliebe?
Tho' he scorns me and ignores me,	Und verbarg mir seine Triebe,
And pretends he has not heard?	Wandte sein Gesicht von mir?
Why then can't he speak a word?	Warum sprach er nicht mit mir?

THE THREE BOYS

We can't tell you, but believe us,	Dieses müssen wir verschweigen,
And we'll gladly take you with us,	Doch, wir wollen dir ihn zeigen!
You will see we don't deceive,	Und du wirst mit Staunen sehn,
For your lover still is true —	Dass er dir sein Herz geweiht,
He will dare to die for you.	Und den Tod für dich nicht scheut.

PAMINA

Lead me there, I long to see him.	Führt mich hin, ich möcht ihn sehen.

THE THREE BOYS

Come with us and do not grieve.	Komm, wir wollen zu ihm gehen.

PAMINA, THE THREE BOYS

Two loving hearts that beat together	Zwei Herzen, die von Liebe brennen,
Are safe from earthly woes forever.	Kann Menschenohnmacht niemals trennen.

117

They need not fear the fires of Hell;
The Gods themselves will guard them
well.

Verloren ist der Feinde Müh';
Die Götter selbst beschützen sie.

Exeunt.

Transformation. Scene Twenty-eight. *Two high mountains. From one mountain, the rushing and roaring of a waterfall may be heard; the other spits out fire. Through a grill in each mountain, the fire and water can be seen — where the fire burns the horizon should be red as hell, while a thick mist lies on the water. There are rocks all over the stage, which is divided into two separate parts, each enclosed within an iron gate. Tamino is lightly clothed, without sandals. Two men in black armour accompany Tamino; on their helmets, flames burn. They read him the inscription, illuminated from within, on a pyramid high up in the centre, above the grills.*

THE ARMED MEN [35]

Man that is born of woman walks thro'
life in shadow,
Yet light and truth may pierce
thro' pain and sorrow.
Man must brave Death, the dread that
haunts him from his birth —
Then he shall find his heaven here on
earth.
Enlightened Man will see truth pure and
whole,
And, finding truth, he shall find his
immortal soul.

Der, welcher wandert, diese Strasse voll
Beschwerden,
Wird rein durch Feuer, Wasser, Luft
und Erden;
[36] Wenn er des Todes Schrecken über-
winden kann,
Schwingt er sich aus der Erde himmelan.

Erleuchtet wird er dann imstande sein,

Sich den Mysterien der Isis ganz zu
weihn.

TAMINO

I'll not fear Death, no man is braver.

In seeking Truth, I'll never waver.
So fling the gates of terror wide:
I'll gladly bear the trials inside.

Mich schreckt kein Tod, als Mann zu
handeln,
Den Weg der Tugend fortzuwandeln.
Schliesst mir die Schreckenspforten auf,
Ich wäge froh den kühnen Lauf.

PAMINA
(from within)

Tamino, wait, oh, wait for me.

Tamino, halt! Ich muss dich sehn.

TAMINO

What was that? Pamina calling?

Was hör ich? Paminens Stimme?

THE ARMED MEN

Yes, yes, you heard Pamina calling.

Ja, ja, das ist Paminens Stimme.

TAMINO, THE ARMED MEN

Thank God, $\begin{Bmatrix} \text{now} \\ \text{for} \end{Bmatrix}$ she may $\begin{Bmatrix} \text{come} \\ \text{go} \end{Bmatrix}$ with $\begin{Bmatrix} \text{me} \\ \text{you} \end{Bmatrix}$

And so as one $\begin{Bmatrix} \text{we'll} \\ \text{you'll} \end{Bmatrix}$ meet $\begin{Bmatrix} \text{our} \\ \text{your} \end{Bmatrix}$ fate,

Though even Death may lie in wait.

Wohl $\begin{Bmatrix} \text{mir} \\ \text{dir} \end{Bmatrix}$, nun kann sie mit $\begin{Bmatrix} \text{mir} \\ \text{dir} \end{Bmatrix}$ gehn,

Nun trennet $\begin{Bmatrix} \text{uns} \\ \text{euch} \end{Bmatrix}$ kein Schicksal mehr,

Wenn $\begin{Bmatrix} \text{gleich} \\ \text{auch} \end{Bmatrix}$ der Tod beschieden wär!

TAMINO

And now, am I allowed to greet her?

Ist mir erlaubt, mit ihr zu sprechen?

THE ARMED MEN

Yes, now you are allowed to greet her.

Dir ist erlaubt, mit ihr zu sprechen!

118

What joy to see $\left\{\begin{array}{l}\text{my}\\\text{your}\end{array}\right\}$ love again.

With her, $\left\{\begin{array}{l}\text{I'll}\\\text{you'll}\end{array}\right\}$ feel no other pain.

A girl who'll brave death by $\left\{\begin{array}{l}\text{my}\\\text{his}\end{array}\right\}$ side.

May surely fill a man with pride.

Welch Glück, wenn wir $\left\{\begin{array}{l}\text{uns}\\\text{euch}\end{array}\right\}$ wiedersehn,

Froh Hand in Hand in Tempel gehn.

Ein Weib, das Nacht und Tod nicht scheut,

Ist würdig und wird eingeweiht.

The door opens; Tamino and Pamina embrace. [37]

PAMINA

Tamino mine! Oh what great joy!

Tamino mein! O welch ein Glück!

TAMINO

Pamina mine! Oh what great joy!
See here the dreaded doorway
Where pain and death may lie.

Pamina mein! O welch ein Glück!
Hier sind die Schreckenspforten,
Die Not und Tod mir dräun.

PAMINA

Our love will find a sure way,
With you I'll live or die.
I'll stay here by your side
And Love shall be our guide.

Ich werde aller Orten
An deiner Seite sein,
Ich selbsten führe dich,
Die Liebe leitet mich.

She takes him by the hand.

Beside our road the wild thorn grows,
But midst the thorn there is a rose.
So take the magic flute and play.
Its sound will guard us on our way.
'Twas carved by Father, in an hour of enchantment
In the deepest forests,
From root and wood of ancient oak —
While lightning carved it, storm clouds broke.
So take the magic flute and play.
Its sound will guard us on our way.

Sie mag den Weg mit Rosen streun,
Weil Rosen stets bei Dornen sein.
Spiel du die Zauberflöte an,
Sie schütze uns auf unsrer Bahn.
Es schnitt in einer Zauberstunde

Mein Vater sie aus tiefstem Grunde
Der tausendhähr'gen Eiche aus,
Bei Blitz und Donner, Sturm und Braus.

Nun komm und spiel die Flöte an,
Sie leite uns auf grauser Bahn.

TAMINO, PAMINA, THE ARMED MEN [38]

$\left.\begin{array}{l}\text{We'll}\\\text{They'll}\end{array}\right\}$ walk unharmed, thro' music's power

$\left.\begin{array}{l}\text{Wir}\\\text{Ihr}\end{array}\right\}$ wandeln durch des Tones Macht,

Thro' deepest night and Death's dark hour.

Froh durch des Todes düstre Nacht!

The doors close behind them. Tamino and Pamina can be seen advancing. The spitting of fire and howling of wind can be heard; at times also the muffled sound of thunder and the rushing of water. Tamino plays his flute [39]. *Drums softly sound. As soon as they emerge from the mountain of fire, they embrace and take up a position in the centre of the stage.*

TAMINO AND PAMINA

We walked unharmed thro' flames of passion,
The temper of our souls was true.
Oh flute, now guard us in this fashion,
Whatever floods of grief may do.

Wir wandelten durch Feuergluten,
Bekämpften mutig die Gefahr.
Dein Ton sei Schutz in Wasserfluten,
So wie er es im Feuer war.

Tamino plays. They are seen to descend and shortly afterwards to come up again. Then a door opens, through which a brilliantly lit temple may be seen. Solemn silence. This vision must be of the utmost splendour. The chorus, accompanied by trumpets and drums, begin to sing.

Oh Gods, we see a blessed sight.
Now man's dark world is filled with
    light.

Ihr Götter! Welch ein Augenblick!
Gewähret ist uns Isis Glück.

CHORUS
(from within)

Rejoice, rejoice, you noble pair.
Your hearts were true, your courage rare!
The prize of virtue now is yours.
Come, see the temple's open doors.

Triumph! Triumph! Du edles Paar!
Besieget hast du die Gefahr,
Der Isis Weihe ist nun dein,
Kommt, tretet in den Tempel ein!

Exeunt

Scene Twenty-nine. *The scene changes to the garden again. Enter Papageno.*

PAPAGENO
(having played a little on his pipes [6]*)* [40]

Papagena! Papagena! Papagena!
Sweetheart, hear me — are you hiding?
It's useless! Ah, she's gone forever.
I should have tried to be more clever.
I had to talk, *had* to talk, I'd not be
    taught.
I must admit it was my fault.
Since I first drank that lovely wine,
Since I first saw that lovely girl,
I cannot rest till she is mine.
My heart's on fire, my heads awhirl.
Papagena! I adore you!
Papagena! I implore you!
It's no use, she cannot hear me;
Now my life is cold and dreary!
Papageno, save your breath —
Farewell, Life and welcome, Death!
I shall hang here on the gibbet
With a rope around my gizzard.
Tired of life and crossed in love,
Farewell, World, I'm off above.
While I lived the girls ignored me:
Now I'm martyred, they'll adore me.
That's enough, I'm going to die —
Lovely ladies do not cry.
But if one of you will have me,
Well, you've one more chance to save me,
Tell me quick, or else I'll go —
Don't be shy, say yes or no?
No one answers: what a silence.
No one, no one loves me.
Not a single lady loves me.
Papageno, give up hope —
You must dangle from a rope.
No. I'll wait a bit, maybe . . .
'Till I've counted one, two, three . . .

Papagena, Papagena, Papagena!
Weibchen, Täubchen, meine Schöne!
Vergebens! Ach, sie ist verloren!
Ich bin zum Unglück schon geboren.
Ich plauderte — und das war schlecht,

Darum geschieht es mir schon recht.
Seit ich gekostet diesen Wein,
Seit ich das schöne Weibchen sah,
So brennt's im Herzenskämmerlein,
So zwickt es hier, so zwickt es da.
Papagena, Herzensweibchen!
Papagena, liebes Täubchen!
's ist umsonst, es ist vergebens!
Müde bin ich meines Lebens!
Sterben macht der Lieb ein End,
Wenn's im Herzen noch so brennt.
Diesen Baum da will ich zieren,
Mir an ihm den Hals zuschnüren,
Weil das Leben mir missfällt;
Gute Nacht, du schwarze Welt.
Weil du böse an mir handelst,
Mir kein schönes Kind zubandelst:
So ist's aus, so sterbe ich,
Schöne Mädchen, denkt an mich.
Will sich eine um mich Armen,
Eh' ich hänge, noch erbarmen,
Wohl, so lass ich's diesmal sein!
Rufet nur, ja — oder nein. —
Keine hört mich, alles stille!
Also ist es euer Wille?
Papageno, frisch hinauf!
Ende deinen Lebenslauf.
Nun, ich warte noch, es sei,
Bis man zählet, eins, zwei, drei.

(he pipes)

One!   Eins!

(he pipes)

Two! [Two is already gone!]   Zwei! Zwei ist schon vorbei.

(he pipes)

Three!   Drei!

Ah, well, that's the end of me.	Nun wohlan, es bleibt dabei!
Since I cannot find my love,	Weil mich nichts zurücke hält!
Cruel world, I'm off above.	Gute Nacht, du falsche Welt.

He prepares to hang himself.

THE THREE BOYS
(descending from above)

Oh, wait, oh, Papageno, that's no way.	Halt ein, o Papageno, und sei klug;
You've only one life, live it while you may.	Man lebt nur einmal, dies sei dir genug.

PAPAGENO

That's very true and nicely spoken,	Ihr habt gut reden, habt gut scherzen.
But don't you see my heart is broken?	Doch brennt es euch wie mich im Herzen,
One day you too will want a wife.	Ihr würdet auch nach Mädchen gehn.

THE THREE BOYS

Well, why not ring the bells you carry?	So lasse deine Glöckchen klingen,
They'll bring the girl you want to marry.	Dies wird dein Weibchen zu dir bringen.

PAPAGENO

I'm such a fool to be so tragic.	Ich Narr vergass der Zauberdinge!
Come on you bells, let's hear your magic.	Erklinge, Glöckenspiel, erklinge!
I long to see my girl again.	Ich muss mein liebes Mädchen sehn.

As he plays the bells, the Three Boys run to their flying machine and help Papagena to dismount. [41]

Now bells, let your music	Klinget, Glöckchen, klinget,
Bring my sweetheart here:	Schafft mein Mädchen her!
Sweet bells, sound your music	Klinget, Glöckchen, klinget,
Make my loved one hear.	Bringt mein Weibchen her!
Now bells, with your music,	*(repeat)*
If my dear girl's near,	
Sweet bells sound your music,	
Make my dear wife hear.	
With your magic music,	
Make my sweetheart hear.	
If she's near,	
Oh bring her here,	
My dearest dear!	

THE THREE BOYS

Now Papageno, turn around!	Nun, Papageno, sieh dich um!

Papageno looks around. Then each plays a comic routine. [42]

PAPAGENO

Pa-Pa-Pa-Pa-Pa-Pa-Papagena!	Pa-Pa-Pa-Pa-Pa-Pa-Papagena!

PAPAGENA

Pa-Pa-Pa-Pa-Pa-Pa-Papageno.	Pa-Pa-Pa-Pa-Pa-Pa-Papageno!

TOGETHER

Pa-Pa-Pa-Pa-Pa-Pa {Papagena! / Papageno!	Pa-Pa-Pa-Pa-Pa-Pa {Papagena! / Papageno!

PAPAGENO

Ah, now shall we live together?	Bist du mir nun ganz gegeben?

	PAPAGENA
Yes, we'll always live together.	Nun bin ich dir ganz gegeben.

	PAPAGENO
Then you'll be my wife for ever?	Nun, so sei mein liebes Weibchen!

	PAPAGENA
Yes, I'll share your life forever.	Nun, so sei mein Herzenstäubchen!

	TOGETHER
We'll live together, in love forever.	*(repeat)*

Oh, what happiness and joy	Welche Freude wird das sein,
If the kindly gods will maybe	Wenn die Götter uns bedenken,
Bless our marriage with a baby,	Unsrer Liebe Kinder schenken,
A little girl or little boy . . .	So liebe kleine Kinderlein!

	PAPAGENO
First send a little Papageno.	Erst einen kleinen Papageno!

	PAPAGENA
Then send a little Papagena.	Dann eine kleine Papagena!

	PAPAGENO
We'll have another Papageno.	Dann wieder einen Papageno!

	PAPAGENA
Then have another Papagena.	Dann wieder eine Papagena!

	PAPAGENO
Papageno, Papageno, Papageno, Papageno.	Papageno, Papageno, Papageno, Papageno.

	PAPAGENA
Papagena, Papagena, Papagena, Papagena.	Papagena, Papagena, Papagena, Papagena.

	TOGETHER
It is the sweetest human pleasure	Es ist das höchste der Gefühle,
To have a dear young	Wenn viele, viele, viele, viele
{ Pa-Pa-Pa-Pa-geno { Pa-Pa-Pa-Pa-gena	{ Pa-Pa-Pa-Pa-geno { Pa-Pa-Pa-Pa-gena
To comfort their old parents' lives.	Der Eltern Segen werden sein.

They hurry off.

Scene Thirty. *Monostatos, the Three Ladies and the Queen of the Night enter stealthily, carrying flaming black torches.* [43]

	MONOSTATOS
We must be silent, silent, silent.	Nur stille, stille, stille, stille!
We're near the inner temple now.	Bald dringen wir im Tempel ein.

	THE QUEEN, THREE LADIES
We must be silent, silent, silent.	Nur stille, stille, stille, stille!
We're near the inner temple now.	Bald dringen wir im Tempel ein.

	MONOSTATOS
But Highness, keep your word. You promised	Doch Fürstin, halte Wort! Erfülle —
I'd have your daughter as my wife.	Dein Kind muss meine Gattin sein.

THE QUEEN

I'll keep my word. As I have promised	Ich halte Wort; es ist mein Wille.
You'll have my daughter as your wife.	Mein Kind soll deine Gattin sein.

THE THREE LADIES

Her child shall be your wife.	Ihr Kind soll deine Gattin sein.

Sounds of thunder and rushing water.

MONOSTATOS

But now I hear a fearful thunder	Doch still! Ich höre schrecklich Rauschen
Of roaring flames and surging waves.	Wie Donnerton und Wasserfall.

THE QUEEN, THREE LADIES

Yes, sound of wind and crashing thunder —	Ja, fürchterlich ist dieses Rauschen
How it re-echoes thro' these caves.	Wie fernen Donners Widerhall.

MONOSTATOS

Now they are met in solemn counsel.	Nun sind sie in des Tempels Hallen.

THE QUEEN, THREE LADIES, MONOSTATOS

Then it is there we'll fall upon them,	Dort wollen wir sie überfallen —
And while they worship their false Lord	Die Frömmler tilgen von der Erd'
We'll rise and put them to the sword.	Mit Feuersglut und mächt'gem Schwert.

THREE LADIES, MONOSTATOS

Thou blazing Queen who rules in might,	Dir, grosse Königin der Nacht,
Now see us take the vengeance of Night.	Sei unsrer Rache Opfer gebracht.

With a very violent chord, thunder and lightning, the scene changes so that the whole stage represents a sun. Sarastro stands on high; Tamino and Pamina are both in priestly robes. On either side of them are the Egyptian priests. The Three Boys hold flowers in their hands.

THE QUEEN, THREE LADIES, MONOSTATOS

Ah God, we're cast down and our glory departs,	Zerschmettert, zernichtet ist unsere Macht,
The bright light of Truth drives its sword thro' our hearts.	Wir alle gestürzet in ewige Nacht.

They sink into the ground.

SARASTRO

The grandeur and glory of truth sheds its light,	Die Strahlen der Sonne vertreiben die Nacht,
Destroyed are the sinful, destroyed is the night.	Zernichten der Heuchler erschlichene Macht.

CHORUS [44]

Hail the Two who triumphed!	Heil sei euch Geweihten!
They dared all for Truth!	Ihr dranget durch Nacht.
Praise the God of Wisdom!	Dank sei dir, Osiris,
See the Truth shining bright!	Dank dir, Isis, gebracht!
For Truth is all-powerful,	[45]Es siegte die Stärke
And Love is his Lord,	Und krönet zum Lohn
And Beauty and Wisdom	Die Schönheit und Weisheit
Shall earn their reward!	Mit ewiger Kron'!

THE END

Discography

In order of UK release. All recordings are in stereo, unless asterisked *, and in German.

Conductor / Company/Orchestra	*Karajan* Vienna Singverein Vienna PO	*Böhm* Vienna Opera & PO	*Fricsay* RIAS Choir Berlin SO	*Klemperer* Philharmonia	*Böhm* Berlin PO	*Solti* Vienna Opera & PO
Tamino	A. Dermota	L. Simoneau	E. Haefliger	N. Gedda	F. Wunderlich	S. Burrows
Pamina	I. Seefried	H. Gueden	M. Stader	G. Janowitz	E. Lear	P. Lorengar
Sarastro	L. Weber	K. Bohme	J. Greindl	G. Frick	F. Crass	M. Talvela
Queen of the Night	W. Lipp	W. Lipp	R. Streich	L. Popp	R. Peters	C. Deutekom
Papageno	E. Kunz	W. Berry	D. Fischer-Dieskau	W. Berry	D. Fischer-Dieskau	H. Prey
Ladies	S. Jurinac	J. Hellwig	M. Schech	E. Schwarzkopf	H. Hillebrecht	H. van Bork
	F. Riegler	C. Ludwig	L. Losch	C. Ludwig	C. Ahlin	Y. Minton
	E. Schurhof	H. Rossl-Majdan	M. Klose	M. Hoffgen	S. Wagner	H. Phimacher
Monostatos	P. Klein	A. Jaresch	M. Vantin	G. Unger	F. Lenz	G. Stolze
Speaker	G. London	P. Schoeffler	K. Borg	F. Crass	H. Hotter	D. Fischer-Dieskau
Priest	E. Majkut	E. Majkut	H. Vandenburg	G. Unger	M. Vantin	K. Equiluz
Papagena	E. Loose	E. Loose	L. Otto	R.M. Pütz	L. Otto	R. Holm
Disc UK Number	SLS 5062 *	GOS501 - 3	2701 015	SLS912	2709 017	SET 479 - 81
Tape Number					3371 - 002	K2A4
Excerpts (Disc)		SDD218			1316440	SET 527
Excerpts (Tape)		SDD218			922 - 014	KSET 527
Disc US Number	SRS63507			S-3651	DG 2709017	LON-1397
Tape Number					3371 - 002	—
Excerpts (Disc)				S 36315	DG 136440	LON 26257
Excerpts (Tape)				8X514-XS - 36315	922014	